I0165750

now

leaving

nowheresville

By
Philip Kobylarz

BLUE LIGHT PRESS ❖ 1ST WORLD PUBLISHING

1ST WORLD
PUBLISHING

SAN FRANCISCO ❖ FAIRFIELD ❖ DELHI

now leaving nowheresville

Copyright ©2014 by Philip Kobylarz

All rights reserved. Printed in the United States of America. No part of this book may be used or reproduced in any manner whatsoever without written permission except in the case of brief quotations embodied in critical articles and reviews. For information contact:

1st World Library
PO Box 2211
Fairfield, Iowa 52556
www.1stworldpublishing.com

Blue Light Press
www.bluelightpress.com
Email: bluelightpress@aol.com

Book & Cover Design
Melanie Gendron

Editing
Kerry Hillis

Cover Photo
Melanie Gendron

Author Photo
Philip Kobylarz

First Edition

Library of Congress Control Number: 2014956743

ISBN 9781421886930

acknowledgements

The Man Who Drove Seeking Autumn, *Green Mountains Review*

Advice, *Tampa Review*

Daybook, the Great Plains, 1867, *Colorado Review*

Lake Shore Drive, *Witness*

At 8,000 Feet, *Blueline*

End of the Great Plains, *Plieades*

Aftermath, *Scrivner* (Montréal)

The Atheist's Club, *The Chimera Review*

Famous Last Words, *Full Circle*

Confessions of an Altar Boy, *The Gihon Review*

Open 24 Hours, *Steam Ticket*
"Me, Her and my Machine" *R-kv-ry*

"Lucinda" *The Iconoclast*

"Transformed, the Office Narcissus" *13ᵗʰ Moon*

"What We Do Beyond" *Lalitamba*, 2008

"The Taste of Neon" 2008

"Aquamarine" *Slab Literary Magazine* 2008

"Voice Mail" *Whiskey Island*

"The Atheists' Club" *Massachusetts Review*

"The Blue Sky" *De La Mancha*

With endless gratitude to Kerry Hillis for
her editing skills and friendship.

table of contents

VERNAL

BOREAL

interlude

AUTUMNAL

INDIAN SUMMER

For Gabriela Kubik's sister, Karina Plotek

"Only the few know the sweetness of the twisted apples."
—Sherwood Anderson, *Winesburg, Ohio*

vernal

NO VACANCY

There is a slight breeze coming in from the northwest, as there usually is, made apparent by a fan blade slowly spinning in the window. Shadows from objects in the room—a plant, a bicycle, a stack of papers—fluctuate on the walls as if surrounded by water. The whole room is flooded by sunlight so bright it's hard to make out the time on the digital clock's readout. Must be later than noon. Under the window, there are screams of children playing some game they invented during the morning hours. They will play and play until interrupted by an ice cream truck's static tune. They will buy ice cream the color of flags, then rest under the shade of an oak tree, left over change silent in their pockets. Above the oak tree, from the room with its plastic roller shade constricted, past the two solitary apartment buildings bordering the river's bank, a hill is gradually darkening. Clouds beyond the hill look like a far-off mountain range dying in the ember glance of late afternoon. There are no mountains for what might as well be continents. The contents of the room are becoming imperceptible and indistinguishable. In intervals of minutes, lights appear in apartments like a gradual Morse code that will, by night, signal an awaited message. Dog barks interrupt and fade as intermittent rain showers would, if the clouds which are rising into anvils, were closer. Birds call dibs on the last of the mulberries on the tree across the street. Mostly robins. An occasional thrush. Smells of sausage frying in beer waft up from the lower level. An oven door squeaks open to reveal its treasure of baked bread tied in a knot. What looks like a figure of a man, but is probably a bent t.v. antenna, is propped stationary on a roof. It might move, might make one gesture, as the light falls. Addresses painted on the curbs are adding themselves up into blocks of unknown symbols, hastily drawn Arabics of calligraphy. The wind coursing through the window is petering out. The blade of the fan drops its guise of a circle unbroken. Moments before the darkness, cracks of light appear through the walls. There is no one in the room.

THE MAN WHO DROVE SEEKING AUTUMN

The man who drove seeking autumn exited from the highway onto an interstate that crossed the river. The river was at full crest; its waters were speeding along almost as fast as his car, currents rushing in a perpendicular route. At the bridge, he pulled over and parked at the shoulder of the road to watch filthy waves lap at concrete supports. A weeded-over path led to an abandoned barn on the banks. He walked it, avoiding tepid puddles. The mosquitoes and gnats attacked his eyes and mouth, attempting to find a nest for the moment. It was getting late in the year and their eggs would have to be laid before the temperatures became any cooler. He brushed them from his face and blew at the lock of hair growing like a stray vine of kudzu from his forehead. Along the way, imperceptible frogs jumped from where his feet might be landing. He could hear the re-entry of their agitated splashes.

The emptied barn held the usual treasures: bricks fired from a local, out-of-business kiln, some planks of rotted wood, pieces of rusted equipment, a mangled construct of barbed-wire fence. In a better day, these things had a use and purpose. Now that memory or lack of it had mislaid them here, they could only accrete the patina of relics. Decades of dust and seasons of mold had claimed them in a tedious sacrifice of inertia. He picked up a railroad spike so rusted that he could have sold it as one of the nails of Christ's cross and tossed it through the window into the river's steady flow. How even iron crumbles when fortified with time.

When he approached his car, he heard voices speaking in conversation filtering out of the windows into the still air. He turned the radio off, not realizing that he had left it on, and got back on the interstate. The traffic was minimal; mostly trucks doing under the limit and tourists seeking the closest bed & breakfast. The days in October had become so obvious: the smell of harvest in the air, the burning of wood piles. The only mystery that remained was the fact that the leaves were still green. They hadn't changed yet, and perhaps they wouldn't this year. Then what would the people of this city, the surrounding rural towns, and the farmers of this sleepy county do?

He passed a cemetery on a hill surrounded by an iron fence as if it needed to keep something out. He had passed this sacred place many times before without ever seeing any visitors. Today there was an old man busying himself with the task of gardening a plot of land. He was pulling weeds and tending a row of snapdragons. The old gentleman looked up and waved to the passing car as if he were interrupted in his work. The man who drove waved back and continued on his way.

On the outskirts of a small town, there was a water tower shaped like a spacecraft. The tiny ladder affixed to its side allowed bored high school kids in the vicinity to climb it and spray paint their logos of wonderment and desire. Of course, the graffiti was incomprehensible and read more like modernized petroglyphs than words in any language. The tower must be the tallest structure in the town of two thousand or so residents. He wondered how the stars looked from this platform on a clear, cold night.

The town itself contained a grain elevator, two bars, and a restaurant that advertised, as its specialty, *Fried Cat-fish*. He was sure the food inside was good; cooked with attention and the skill that monotony bred, but he wasn't particularly hungry and didn't feel up to the small talk that would invariably accompany a stranger taking a meal this far off of the main thoroughfare. Maybe another day he would stop there, as he had told himself a hundred times before.

Passing through the business district, he found himself again in the fields abandoned to crops, mostly wheat and corn, swaying like metronomes in the wind. The scarecrows, confined to open prisons behind barbed-wire fences, waited patiently in crucifixion. Some of them stared at their companions across the road, wearing torn flannel shirts. Their language was one of gestures brought about by gusts of air. Others looked on nonchalantly, lacking heads.

The man who drove did not miss the comforts of his house that was tucked away between some hills on the outskirts of the city. The city was twenty-five miles away, according to the mileage markers posted on the signs he had to read in the rearview. His wife and child might be wondering were he was at this time of the evening. Even he didn't know.

The man who drove seeking autumn was beginning to lose the feel of the road underneath him. It was as if the car had begun to float, at first inches, then, feet above the yellow-lined route. He accelerated to eighty-five, then ninety miles an hour. There was nothing that would interrupt his path– no cars, no school crossings. Perhaps a stray skunk or opossum might intersect with his trajectory and create a dull thump under his chassis, but this was not an immediate concern. One could only be so careful in life, and tragedies could only be assumed and waited for without the weight of consternation.

Dusk was approaching and the horizon was dyeing itself pink. In a few moments, he would have to put the headlights on, and probably, the heat. The air was cooling at a proportional rate to the light's diminishing. But in the last minutes of the sinking day he could still see that the leaves of the trees—maple, sugar oak, poplar—were as green as the grass of summer. He wondered why this was so, being so late in the year. He wondered if they would ever change again. He didn't remember the science behind the phenomenon, though he had read it somewhere once. Maybe it was due to global warming, maybe the weather patterns for this region had been altered forever. Maybe the earth's axis had tilted a few degrees. This single mystery of life eluded him. So he kept on driving, slowing down some at county road intersections.

What his wife and child were doing at this time was what he began to think about. How many times he had come home from work and there they would be, on the sofa, watching television. When they watched the news, his daughter would sit behind her mother and brush her mother's hair. While she brushed, sometimes precariously, she would ask questions about the reports. Where was this place, where was that? Why were these people fighting those? Her mother would patiently answer, never taking her eyes off the screen. He wondered whether or not they would be wondering about him. If he were to ask them about the leaves, they would probably look out the window and wait for him to answer his own question.

But he had no answers. The pine trees that sheltered the fewer and fewer farmhouses he passed would never change their color unless they were dying. They are like umbrellas that last forever, he thought. Accompanied by these roads that also lasted forever, the pines were his only consolation. When he was forced to slow down at the eventual stop sign, he could see in the light of his brights bundles of dead leaves from last autumn collected in heaps in the grass beyond the gravel shoulder. These leaves could be collected and be redistributed to front lawns and gutters of his city if fall were not to come this year. He could smell them burning in bundles on street corners and in vacant lots. How he would miss that this year.

A year among years without an autumn. How the thought depressed him, even though a respite from nature's death might be enlivening for others. If autumn had forgot to visit his corner of the country, would winter refuse to make her resplendent white appearance too?

At a railroad crossing he slowed to a standstill. He stopped the car and entered into the evening air. He walked to the tracks and placed his ear on the rail. He thought he heard a distant rumbling, but it was only a semi approaching from the opposite direction of the road. Through the trees and weeds that had grown to twice the size of a man, he saw a lonely train depot, probably no longer in use. The name of the hamlet it once supplied was barely legible, labeled on its side in paint that had peeled away. The words looked like a cursive attempt at Sanskrit. There was a yellow light bulb flickering in its hanging fixture, as if powered by the electricity of past crowds the depot once held. The townspeople might have decided to leave it on as a signal for transients. They were welcome here as long as they didn't come into the town.

He returned to the car and continued on. He couldn't be more than fifteen miles from the big river that separated his state from the next. The night barges would be slowly moving along its banks. The night barges would be bringing goods from the north, from Michigan and Canada. They might even be importing autumn on their wide beds, tucked under spreads of canvas like blocks of dry ice that seep cool streams of crystallized air.

He thought about the river's banks. He knew the smell as well as that of cut grass on summer afternoons. How the few unlucky fish and pieces of litter would be floating in the swell. And the sounds of eager birds circling overhead. Empty beer cans filled with silt and backwater. Of these things he was sure. As sure as the encroaching dawn.

He entered the river city. Trucks were unloading their cargoes of frozen food and freshly baked loaves of bread. The streetlights were flickering off in the oncoming, light blue advent of morning. He found a park along the river. He parked and got out. Maybe the trees along the banks had changed, were changing. Autumn, like a stray barge, could be seeping into this part of the country from the northern climes. Perhaps it would bleed from the rivers into the land-locked regions like the unwanted waters of a flood. This was his best guess.

The woods were a line of unbroken silhouette. Fog hung in the air like ghost lakes above pools and eddies. He threw his keys into the river in a sudden splash that gave way to one large and one small concentric circle. He would wait until the barely perceptible tide and vagrant waves brought them back to the rocky shore. He could hear the waters lapping at the outcropping of stones on the banks.

Here, he would wait patiently for autumn. Those who missed him would, he hoped, patiently wait for his return and he would enter the city, his city, in the full regalia and fanfare of fall. Autumn would be trailing him in a blast of cool air at his back, blowing his hair forward like a flame of feathers. He would pull red and orange and auburn leaves from the trees and pass them out as if it were he who was the emissary of the dying season. He would introduce autumn to all he knew and they would praise him for it. His clothes would smell of smoke and burnt kindling and his hair might even be a lighter shade of brown.

He would wait at this slow moving river until he spotted the first yellow leaf. Perhaps this was why the season had not yet come—there was no one to properly greet it. For winter had its Jack Frost, but autumn was alone. He would wait. He would wait for autumn. He would wait for autumn thinking of home.

FISHING FOR TELEVISION

"Got a story that ain't got no moral, let the bad guy win every once in a while"
—the Spinners

Because I live in a valley surrounded by pointy mountains, rows of rusty knife blades, a pyramidal series of bonsai gardens created by an artist whose underlying themes are obviously chaos and desolation (they taught us how to find underlying themes in college), I cannot receive what is everyone's basic right in America: free television.

A thin signal flows into the old fashioned rabbit ears, a relic in itself, or themselves—basically it's a glorified coat hanger taped to a clock radio circa nineteen eighty one. Early, early Etruscan art. What the beautiful people are doing in the fresco space of the screen, however flat or round it is up to you. Today it's mostly pornography or sports (not necessarily in that order), the recent political scandal, or a decade's worth of murder.

The news relays the choice topic du jour: the fuckedupidness of the Middle East. I guess they forgot it was once a holy land. Topic two is always death in its more glorious forms. Always lots of gore and guts just like in the scariest of our hyperviolent scary movies, full of nightmares beyond the realm of abhorrence that we are encouraging our children to soon dream. They'll know how it was. The hell of the 21st century. Yippee!

But there's only really one story. She's dead. The modern incarnation of the 50 foot tall woman. Yes, indeed, Anna is dead.

Our nightmares, however, aren't dreamt anymore. They're what's happening in meaty real time on teevees, ubiquitously showing war war war war war war war war and war. And we don't really have to fight them, we just have to watch. We only have to press the Nielsen button, the old poll, the next poll. Those polls and not the kind girls dance and spin on. It's the only relevant ballet that's left.

The war doesn't matter anymore, The reason is simple.

She's dead.

The hottest reality t.v. show is the one that really doesn't have a goal, no winners, only bloody melodrama that no one even cares about not even the people who think they are reality movie stars. No million dollar prize, maybe a spot in an Adam Sandler featurette or Dr. Pepper commercial. Some such prize that amounts to freakin' nothing and the fuckin' taxes that have to be paid on it. It's all an old Coke bottle top that promises something exactly like thirst. So drink up while you can even if it makes you puke.

And we puke a lot. Or we feel like it. Or we take a host of prescription drugs that prevent it from ever happening.

Day 2: Diary of the New Show

It's us to us, we the people, we the real people of the crazy dream of coolness as life. We want to buy the ultimate freedom on QVC because we know its only going to be there for a limited time. It doesn't matter what the cost. We have cards for that.

Instructions: all it takes is the perfect movie plot, created in storyboards totally elementized (the genre to be decided at a later date) that includes murder, sex, aliens, and a great Costa del Sol locale, sun drenched bikini-ed Spanish babes and the world's best tequila imported from Mexico.

The story of all stories.

The best advice is not to wonder what Theodore Kaczynski mused as he was losing his mind in a Waldenesque cabin enveloped by northwestern white pine on the border of nowhere and nowhere. Yeah, it's o.k. to write each other vapid e-mails of anonymity, of emotional *sturm und drang*, but every once in a while, actually write it down. Paper, ink, that sort of thingy. Read the Randy Weaver book over and over again. Have nightmares of robots busting out your windows with duct-taped guns in their hands because if you do they will be true.

Armageddon– part 832, chapter nine, the end of the end ending.

I like the city to stay awake for me. I enter what you call sleep and I monitor how eveningtude unveils her brunette locks by walking around the country club in which I live and gazing nonchalantly into windows that the rich feel no reason to cover in drapes. They are rarely doing anything more than watching t.v or solemnly drinking booze and watching t.v. or sitting in a room in which a t.v. is on but they are looking in another direction thinking about watching t.v. or what will come on next.

After I Heard Anna Had Died

Here is what happened. I saw some people either fucking or committing murder. I couldn't quite tell. They were moving wildly, muscles flexing, heads, one head with a mane of hair thrown back, the electric eels of flesh and soft lighting, a painting fell from the wall.

Here's what anyone has to know about winters here: there isn't much to do. Sure, there's skiing but when the temperature is below zero, it feels like your face is being peeled off by acid. And what is skiing anyway but falling down a mountain while trying to not kill yourself or crack a rib. So you do this: brave the elements while walking around a rich neighborhood/golf course/serendipitous park combination and you look in windows. The ultra rich, as we all know, never pull their shades because they like to show off their wealth and furniture ordered from the best catalogs. Floral prints are always big. Stuff made out of glass that should never be.

Why the rich have no class has something to do with Americans' displacement from Europe. In this neighborhood built on a gently undulating plane that is meandered in half by a small river and stitched in by 6,000 plus foot mountains, there are numerous Kokopellis. They adorn houses and mailboxes and I'm sure serve as interior knick knacks.

One barren mountain that juts into the sky like an unsharpened meat cleaver where no humans ever go is named Indian Peak and that must be the inspiration. Native American culture exists only as a smoke-filled casino of one-armed bandits that lies on the north side of a highway that bisects the state and leads to two ends of nowhere. Remember the crying Native American who laments pollution? Well, here, the tears have all dried up and no one ever has to see their suffering. And the city in which I live is named after a Chief.

The night I went out to see the murder/romantic interlude was crystal clear with meteors flying overhead. The geese leave green Cheetos of shit all over the golf course that you inevitably walk in and trek behind you like vegetal footprints. In the distance there is a rumbling of a train that is more so felt than heard. Who knows what they hold as there are only a few stores in town owned by the big chains and no restaurants worth mentioning.

Voyeurism is a last resort when there is nothing better to do. This explains all the sex on the internet. It's all American sex and there are thousands of other countries but we do it best. Or we do it the worst and try hard to be romantic about it. These are the facts and I'm sticking to them. I am no criminal, just an observer of how weird life has become past the turn of the 21st century.

Isn't the Sky the Weather Channel?

Every day is a gray one. The weather here is ominous, especially if it indicates anything about the afterlife. Half of the country is steamy and warm in the middle of winter, the other is freezing its ass off. Or course, I'm in the freezing part– weather so cold that people don't even want to have sex. The clouds hang above the mountains and loom over them like hunchback of non-existent Notre Dames. However, despite of the horribly frozen weather that makes the thin veneer of snow crunch and whine like Styrofoam cutting Styrofoam underfoot, that couple on a wintery Thursday night were going at it like rabbits in a warm den. Or someone was murdering someone.

Here are the facts. I saw a struggle. A painting fell off the wall. I think I heard the telephone ringing, unanswered. Or was it my imagination? Am I tainted by so many CSI programs and Datelines about death? Late, sleepless nights reading entries in Crimelibrary.com. Who knows? I know what I saw. Two naked people writhing like snakes. He was pulling her hair and her arms were reaching behind trying to strike him. The lights went out and I heard the sounds of something hitting the walls. That's when I ran. I ran under the shining stars above, entering into the puffs of breath that froze immediately in the frozen air. I ran because I felt guilty. I ran home and sat in a room and wondered.

The whatever-I-saw-happening still can't take away the fact that she is dead and moldy but she still lives in radio broadcasts about her and her John Redcorn-like mythical son that just might be true and the thousands of men and pilots of industry that boinked her but couldn't touch the barely real thing she kept inside like a splinter from the True Cross. Some early morning a.m.s will be like this for everyone: the rantings of cable, a thin trickle of a river spilling by over well washed white bread loaves of rocks, the scent of a rattling air conditioner unit flowering the air concrete block clean, and the memory of homeless people sleeping territorially sleeping under lights in a dry basin of a city park in Tucson, AZ. Remembering this in Boise, Idaho on a warm March night. Places she has never been, until now. With me, in memorium.

She weighed 178 pounds when she died. No one cried when she died. People heard it broadcast on t.v. as they scarfed down Kentucky Fried Chicken and they thought for a moment, between swallows of industrial strength mashed potatoes and coleslaw that it was a shame, then they took a sip of cherry vanilla Pepsi.

In the newspaper on Sunday, glorious Sunday when the rain starts and stops and the sun comes out to christen the mountains in halo drapes of yellow then gold then revealing bronze extra gleam, I saw the report that ends the story. So much of the news is about ended stories.

Two people were cited by the police department for disturbing the peace. The old couple neighbors who with their skinny scared Labrador that barks at anything called the neighborhood watch, they had heard some noises, maybe a robbery, and the police were then called because we do have a 9-11 service so why the heck not use it? The horny older couple didn't get cited with a ticket but the police did come out and they pretty much saw the same thing I saw although in a different position (we can only wonder) and from a totally different perspective. And they probably lingered more because they had the right to.

Here is the moral of the lesson as all stories are supposed to have them. Watch how much fun you have because at the height of ecstasy, the cops can come a knocking and you are being watched by everyone and nothing you do is private and she is dead and there are legions of Marilyn Monroe worshippers but none, less me, who are truly, truly devoted to her memory and for it, and the cult of my others, namely, you the reader, are condemned to a darkest sulphuric realm of hell: an internet memorial webpage.

The new infinity.

Guess what? The new telephones books have arrived in their bright yellow bags and no one absolutely even gives a shit.

OPEN 24 HOURS

The skeleton sat at the orange counter of the donut shop with its head bowed over a cup of coffee, its skull in its bony hands. Refuse littered the hosed-down streets and people trickled out of the dark alleys to find their cars or apartments that they rented for the weekend. The skeleton looked as if it were waiting out a migraine, though 4:30 a.m. might be a little too early to be suffering the consequences of a white night. Masculinity could be assigned to his figure by the fraying leather shoes poking out from under his costume. A kind of get-up you rarely see anymore. It fit his body snugly: white lines on a puppeteer's black velvet pajama, capped off with a tawdry plastic mask. It was only the beginning of the night in a town filled with party goers, cops on horseback, and the siren scream of ambulances. Horse shit steamed in the gutters like freshly baked baguettes.

Hours ago, when the hoards were parading and the gaudily clad women on the balconies were dancing and raising their blouses to expose already hardened nipples to night air, he was singing along with the mayhem too. He had fallen in love an innumerable number of times but nothing coalesced from his vagrant desires other than some healthy flirting and speculative innuendo. Sex was not the real reason for his journey this far southward, though the prospect of it would most likely do wonders for his accumulating tension and the pain he looked to be closely guarding in the little corner store lit with too bright fluorescent light. The donut shop was occupied by himself and a bag lady or at least a woman dressed like one. She was looking out the plate glass window and tapping the ashes of her cigarette into a creased soda pop can.

Was it only a week ago when he decided to pack up the remains of his existence two days before the expiration of his lease to try to find a job, a place, some friends in this queer and out of the way location? He wasn't sure about the specifics of time. It had felt like months that he had been uprooted and alone in this city of thousands. He had been kicking around the idea of leaving his dental practice and going back to school or freelancing the odd job market until he could satisfy his wanderlust and take up in an apartment. The daily routine of meeting strangers, learning their occupations and hobbies, then intimately fondling their most private and unique orifice left him with a dulled outlook on life. But teeth are bones and this was something he couldn't seem to get out of his head.

Cleopatra

The bag lady stepped out of the drugstore, fingers poking from of her one glove that she found sticking out of a mailbox on Franklin Street. She had managed to scrounge up enough change to buy some cigarettes and a candy bar– her dinner for the evening. Her existence was metered by the rising and falling of the sun and by the steady march of tourists along the streets. They seemed to pick up in numbers near the city's closing time. Her daily wandering was delineated by landmarks such as mailboxes, coffee houses with their intermittent, odd hours, Catholic churches that from time to time sponsored free meals, and parks and squares that occasionally had open-air festivals where there would be crowds preoccupied with buying trinkets and food. People who would almost always be oblivious to the change and small bills that would find freedom in the uneventful moment of transaction from pocket to vendor or wallet to hand. These were the gestures of her sustenance. Trinkets and food were all people wanted anyway.

She mostly collected things. Aluminum cans and empty liquor bottles of course, always a dependable staple. Her resolute scanning of the ground found her such items as gold-plated charm bracelets, hotel keys, notes in cursive posted to doors and blown off, even compacts and baseball caps. She kept her treasures in a plastic shopping bag that she would hide outside the few businesses and shops in which she could find the courage to seek refuge. The glove she had found today was in perfect condition, only two fingers of it missing.

Shangri-la

Sir Thomas Elroy, honorable Knight of the Round Table, clanked into Joe's Tavern on Paris Road amidst the din of a television broadcasting a basketball game. His princess had excused herself of his company to freshen up in the maids' room while he ordered two glasses of ale to keep the chemical festivities flowing in his brain. The dance that had come to a head had finally run into the wee hours and they made their departure before the city had closed down for good. They had an hour drive home for which he would have to remove his very expensive rented suit of armor and in which he was beginning to feel comfortable. The rush of isolation, anonymity, and power he was enjoying would also dwindle back into a stream of reality that would sink in after he finished his last glass of beer. His maid's dress had gotten quite stained while she danced and whirled her silks among the partygoers in the ballroom. There was a treacherous cognac blotch in the shape of Africa near the frills about her waist which would probably cost them a pretty penny to remove. As she came back to the table, her eyes acknowledged the imperfection as well as his thought on the matter and she shrugged and shook a dash of salt into her beer. She sipped at her elixir and twirled the locks of her auburn curls between her fingers adorned with clear nail polish and plastic rings. She glanced at the digital clock blinking behind the bar and suggested that they begin their journey home. Sir Thomas agreed, attempting to check the hour by raising his forearm to observe his watch that for some reason he wore and could feel on his wrist. Although, he begged of his companion, he would need a shot of java before tackling the highway. She consented in expectation of the none too distant moment when she, the not quite virgin princess and her errant-knight, would soon be free from the ravages of the feast and could, with much clamor and strain, denude.

Inshallah

The single naked buttock of the light bulb illuminated Raymond's loft overlooking the triangular, iron-fenced park. His interior decorating was as sparse as the lighting: two movie posters he found in the garbage can in an alley and some photos torn from the newspaper, taped to the refrigerator. Along the walls painted white for nearly the fifteenth time, (each layer visible in the cracks around the window panes), and about the varnished wood floors, were stacks of encyclopedias that were his in the meantime of possible, but improbable, transaction. He had ten collections of Britannica to sell in a month. He also had a telephone at the foot of his futon and a box of Indian cigarettes that sported an effigy of Ganeesh the elephant. Tonight, with nothing else to do, he would page through the telephone book in hopes of locating a few choice neighborhoods in which he could solicit come morning. The radio was turned on to an all-night talk show whose participants were discussing the fate of wooden roller coasters in the northeast. He cracked open one of the beautifully bound volumes and began reading about an endangered species he had never heard about: the narwhal.

Pegasus

The mutt, half schnauzer/half unknown, ran from its owner at the sight and smell of a pretzel thrown to the ground on the other side of Canal street. Dragging its leash behind, it instinctively knew there were no cars coming, and bolted. It was hungry and this hunger was liberation. The pretzel even had some mustard dried in a blob on the plastic wrap it was enmeshed in, which the dog greedily licked up. It ate so fast that it vomited the meal three blocks down the street, but the dinner was gratifying nevertheless. The tags on its collar jingled as it traipsed down the street not knowing where it was going, just enjoying the sounds and odors of an area defiled by humans. There were the scents of piss in every sewer much like around the base of every tree in the park. There were more partially eaten morsels near garbage cans and empty containers of sweet and sour liquids on every street corner. A paradise for a highly evolved nose.

Where to go. Where did the stray cats it had seen prowling through the back yard sleep at night? Why were the streets wet when there wasn't the tang of rain's iodine in the air? And why were the rare clumps of grass and bushes in this part of the neighborhood locked in cages? Without a master to gesture the answers, it didn't know. It would have to read the subtle signs of abandon. A traffic light blinking red. Litter and leaves blowing at random intervals through the streets. A bus's breaks hissing with the release of air. The ringing of a bell down the street seemed to signal something as a human exited from the building. The lights inside the building lit the sidewalks and the scent of food wisped out. It must be someone's home.

The dog walked toward it, lured by its possibility and goaded by the strange sound of metal clanking on the pavement behind it, then voices. Stopping for a moment to look behind, it saw the silhouette of a human, but the shape was shining, looking like it was made from of the skin of a car. When it approached the light, it found a window with people inside. No couch, no carpet, no fireplace. There was a woman like the ones it saw sleeping in the alleys, a young human with its face in a big book, and near her, a dead human that the others ignored. The armored one with his mate had passed the dog with the woman making kissing noises at it. The bell of the door masked under the sound of metal on metal. The dog sat for a moment waiting for a gesture from any of them, smelled something good, scratched its ear, then, with a ringing of its collar, was gone.

THE TASTE OF NEON

She was the unadopted queen of Memphis, Tennessee, wicked little town beside a lazy chocolate river. How was her royalty ascertained, if I may use one of my few fifty dollar words? A poll. Not the shiny kind girls slide down, after wiping them with sweaty Elvis towels. A poll taken at the local bar, the Killibrew, substantiated by hearsay on campus (the university was just down the other side of the railroad tracks) and buzzwords humming in the back rows of the three star strip joint on the outskirt of town.

A word of warning about that exotic locale: to sum it up tersely, plush. Or maybe, plushville. It is pure bright green velour with orange drapes and red carpet. Oh sure it has cages, the lights of a so-so 70s disco, mindlessly expensive beer, and loud thumping music that stays in your ears early into your cotton-mouthed, hung over and twisted about your throat and waiste morning after. You wish for lipstick traces but they never appear.

The furniture: lounge style sofas with ottomans (not matching) and vaguely Vegas in aspiration. A Ka'aba of a stage in the middle of one big dark room that feels like an unconscious ready to be filled with desire. Darker nooks and corners where who knows what is going on. A special and unassuming lap dance room where things are taken off, soiled, and put back on gingerly without any aplomb at all. And best of all, big private bathrooms with stalls that have doors where a guy or girl can step back, sit down, and take a breather from it all. Cigarette smoke curls under its closed saloon door.

Don't even get me talking about the girls. And that's girls with a tongue-y plural "zzzz-zuh". There are too many in this world for all the men like me. Tall. Short. Some skinny as boys. Some not so skinny at all. Any flavor of hair or racial inkling. And many mixtures, like unheard of cocktails. Big balconies and small. Ditto for the derrieres. An endless array of natural and not so natural tattoos. Flesh candy for the soul.

The one thing that unites their differentness is their level of fine-osity. The girls are something else– reminders what clothes are for.

Clothes keep us civilized. They are not the expected tribes of trailer trash before sweetcakes and fried pies turn them into fat ass Oprah-watching hair gettin' done house cows. They're imported from the big cities that surround: southern belles from Hotlanta and the small easy of Louisville. Sure they all love country and you know what, ain't doing a redneck the whiteman's cheapest thrill?

But I digress. And diversion was the Queen's most effective tactic. Back again to the pit stop of the strip joint whose name is so well ingrained in the psyches of the local clergymen and politicians I cannot name nor fictionalize for real fear of retribution. It was there where I met her highness in a haze of 100s smoke and nearly tepid Budweiser.

Cheryl would and could have been an employee there because she was so Cheryl-ine. If it's curves a woman is supposed to have and effortlessly keep under some sort of control within the bounds of undergarments and such, then flaunt like there is a nation-wide dearth of pillows and pin cushions, then she knew how to work fabric like the Irish speak English. She is an architectural blend of skinny and round in all the right places and some of the wrong. Long auburn hair even if it wasn't that way at birth, and a face that dared billboards to do it justice.

The problem was that, boy oh boy, she knew this. She knew her own temperature. Hot enough to melt kidney stones. Any woman who orders only mixed drinks, and usually Cosmopolitains at that, knows a little something about airs and how to put them on. Couldn't hold it against her though because she has a brain behind all her glossy purple sparkling lip gloss. And what a cup full of top ramen it is.

What are the clichés? That they can make up their faces but not their minds. That they choose men with as much insight as they select nail polish. That they are highly suceptible to sweetalk, even if it tastes of saccharine on the tongue. That they will put out gratefully on the upteenth date if you play your cards well.

Not so with Cheryl. She can engage and disengage a serious talker into and out of conversations on flower cultivation, the relative spiciness of foods, great books of literature she has never read, how bowling can be an erotic sport, the way certain words feel on the gums, narcolepsy as an art and perhaps even craft, how men and women become the same creatures in the bathroom, the theory and use of various types of furniture, how time does not exist and the watch she has to prove it, when it can be publicly appropriate to emit intestinal gas, why the stars it seems have no color, what the five best cities are in America rather than Europe, how shoes make a man or woman, the inherent meaning attributed to great bodies of water, the reason why birds rarely feather their nests with feathers, what it is exactly street signs convey to the perceptive reader, the relative sadness of all state-sponsored holidays especially Christmas and Thanksgiving, why people have and don't have children, time-tested tactics for appearing in doorways, how hairstyles communicate desire, where and where not to burst out in song, how flying a kite can enhance one's dreams, why being single is the only domain for those addicted to others, and where the best bars are with a list of reasons to frequent them, tipping generously and happily on the way to the next.

And there's always a next one with her. Only at dimly lit venues, in comfortable chairs, at wooden tables that aren't quite clean enough to eat off of, can she, being interrupted only by a maitron emptying her brimming ashtray, speak unhingedly about almost anything under the sun. A barfly of a most resplendent hue, she nevertheless carries a furrowed brow of someone who's never quite sure she can cover her tab.

The one night she lost track of her fluid intake without ingesting the least bit of food, and excused herself from the table of her make-shift friends, no one thought much of it. A nose powdering session, no doubt, or a check on the thin skein of makeup beautiful women for some damn reason deign to mask their souls with, she got up and left us, heading straight for the ladies, as she called it, loo.

We, an irregular cast of locals and misfits, carried on fine without her, telling raucous jokes and improvising our own. It was a hodgepodge group of familiars: people who knew each other as classmates, buddies who worked at crappy deep fried restaurants, the odd house painter who'll show up anywhere pre-soused, and the conversation began to dwindle when there was no pretty vase of flowers to hold our collective gaze. Where did you go Cheryl?

Another tight-jeaned bar kitty left our table to look for our Queen and she too stayed in the john a queerfully long time. When the redhead returned alone, she brought bad news that led to a party's end tolling.

Cheryl had found a cozy corner, hunched over the furthest most toilet, and had puked her little pretty guts out. It was only ten thirty. This meant the inevitable.

She would need a ride home.

As resident Prince Valiant of that particular evening, it was my duty– the unnamed narrator– and innocent not yet drunk bystander, to make sure she got home alive and in full possession of her vehicle. There is a fine, blurry line between gentleman and taxi driver. I could tightrope it. On tiptoes.

The drive to chez elle was bumpy, alcohol magnified, and not without obstacles that needed to be swerved: sewer grates and potholes mainly. Cheryl, partially collapsed in the passenger's seat, tried to find some sort of song on the radio that might bring her reeling mind to sober attention. There was nothing but hard-banging rap, liquidy wailing blues that had the effect of putting one even deeper under the flow, and plaintive classical.

Her small, mumbly talk centered on herself and how'd she'd never get a man if she kept up this kind of behavior and what would others think of her? A lightweight, a floozy, a thimble belly? Myself, driver and guide into her perilous inebriation, took the silent route out. I listened. I listened for my very life.

Never had I been attracted to her so strongly until that night of her drunken urban disability. Something about her state of helplessness aroused my curiosity and my lower chakra blood levels. Can't explain it, don't want to. It was maybe the sight of her black pantyhosed ankles meeting the tops of her Prada shoes and her utter inability to move her too long feet. Or how her shoulders collapsed and tucked in bird-like in momentary ruin and forced the slenderness and width of her back to be exposed in all its fleshy, sexy flatness. This was a posture and presentation she'd never let fly when she was aware, awake and

31

drinking, thinking of the next quasi-intellectual thing to say during barroom blabbering.

Oh the thought of spoiling her.

God was with us that night because no cop would kill this fantasy. I used to pray as a kid so I had to have earned some damn karma. As I pulled into her driveway, and she gave directions relatively well, I saw she lived in a flower garden, in the hippest part of town. A bright blue house that resembled a Hansel and Gretel cottage resting atop a miniature botanic garden. She had probably paid someone to plant it for her. To imagine her on her hands and knees with goofy white gardening gloves, holding a trowel and a flower bulb, wiping away perspiration-y wet locks of hair from about her eyes was too much for even a reasonable man to bear. Sometimes the mind works too much.

I escorted her swaying, tipsy rack out of her own vehicle and we were both amazed she didn't add anything to the easy to clean vinyl interior. Barely able to find her keys, she handed me a whole fist of them before she took a catnap at the foot of her door, laying with her legs splayed out like a scarecrow's.

"Just get me in", she whispered.

Desperately.

I found the magic key, clicked open the door, and was met by one very hungry cat, a sad dog locked in a cage, and an artfully decorated house that smelled as if it hadn't been recently lived in.

She got up with my help and plodded into the kitchen, heading straight for the refrigerator to concoct a glass of bottled water and some fizzy powder and Pepto Bismal all mixed together like the inside of her stomach: a remedy for her condition. I lit up a smoke on the porch and opened the door to the dog prison so he could take a whiz in the flowers. Then I joined him.

A shriek came from inside. Cheryl was watching us from her bedroom window. I could see she was lying on her bed, on her stomach, her legs in the air and her pants down around her ankles, a ball of flannel pyjamas in her arms, and her eyes on what I had pointing in my hand. I mouthed the taste of the silent word "sorry".

So what would any guy do in this scenario? Probably not this: walk through the portal, into the living room, turn on a blues station, yell to her "go to sleep, NOW!", as I closed the door behind me. I had seen her behind and it was manna. Before exiting stage left, I, on a post-it note, wrote my e-mail address and stuck it to a book on her coffee table. A book about desserts. This, to me, became the symbol of her ass: and the sight of it burned into my memory forever.

It's now three nights later that I'm recounting this blurb of a lame story. Instead of checking my e-mail every twelve minutes, I'm writing this for no reason whatsoever. I have the radio on. The Bobby Blue Bland is putting me to sleep with the assistance of a half full, always optimistic bottle of rum tucked in between my legs. Got this too: my purpley thoughts for our Queen, her lost cat that I just remembered she mentioned, and the cats we hung with who are probably at some bar drinking somewhere and talking about us and what I dreamt we did. Best thing I have and will forever own is this one for sure certainty raining through my drunkened, thick skull and racing my pulse like a chunk of bad cocaine:

she will never, ever, write me.

SMILE CAPITOL OF THE WORLD

The given nickname of Pocatello, Idaho

The day I saw a UFO I knew I had to quit my job. It was that simple. As simple as a bright light hovering over a 6,700 foot dun-colored mountain at 4:38 a.m. Most of the really important things that happen in this life happen when it's dark out. Pitch black.

The mountain stood at the end of my street on the outskirts of a long forgotten college town in southeastern Idaho. This geographic location meant that the name of the peak– Chink's– could be a blatant racial slur and there wasn't anyone for deserts in the distance in any direction who would ever care or feel an inkling of shame about it. As long as they kept cranking out mediocre Mu Shu Beef at Wang Lin's grease pit on 4th Street, all was good.

It is a damn tall mountain, too, as big as the mythical South's Smokies, but this one is burnt by the sun to look like a multi-layered potato. Its parsley sprigs are juniper trees and it has some crazy stubble of antennae on its head. It also, in the right light, can look like a deflated beehive. Or failed pizza dough.

But it wasn't any aerial lights that were shining that fateful day in June when I took the dog out for her morning crap. There was a glowing orb, a halo with no hole, and it hung there shimmering, but not like a star. It pulsated as if it were beckoning to me in some sort of Morse code language of blink– glowing and spurting out tongues of energy. An otherworldly form of gesturing. Like it desperately wanted to tell me something. And that something was that I was ruining my life.

A so-called rational person might be inclined to say I was seeing things due to my tenuous existence on this ball of life known as the Earth. Sure, I am neither astrophysicist nor an M.D. but I am, or was, a teacher of fellow humans. I knew things. Important things.

My gig was that of an instructor at an English teaching school associated with a real life university. I taught the mechanics of grammar and the art of speech to twenty-somethings from Saudi Arabia, South Korea, Japan, and Taiwan. They loved and revered me and I was the kind of person who would never do them wrong or sell them untrue information. I was an educator and self-proclaimed skeptic of false prophecies. I was a sort of secular Mormon prophet. Only without the harem.

What can anyone or I really tell anyone about foreigners? They are the true aliens. The weirdest thing about them is their food and the way it smells. Of course, they think the same about hot dogs and chalupas. They're only foreign because they so want to be like us, empty headed and American, addicted to sugar and unrealizable dreams. And the sad thing is that sometimes they think and see themselves as lizard-skinned, cat-eyed, creatures from a distant nebula just because they aren't us and will never be admitted into the club. The funny thing is how they think we're the standard of normality. We, the people who put cheese on everything to make it, finally, good.

The English language school sat in a semi-decrepit former office or even bank building at the end of the two mountain ranges that hemmed in the town, at the open arms of a naturally formed Y of habitation and occasional moose-wandered wilderness. Within its prison-like shell, in a yellow brick perfunctory box renovated to look like a modern office, there is a room that contains hundreds upon hundreds of taxidermied birds. Owls spreading their wings stacked on red tail hawks stealthily searching for prey. This room was the first clue.

What we actually taught under the guise of language acquisition was this: how to smile constantly, how to pretend to be happy, how to don't worry in the artful deceit of please, at all times, be fake and have a nice day. Since the syllabi (or alibis) and the objectives all came from a series of anonymous, apocryphal corporate writers, this was quite an easy task.

Coincidentally there are as many theories about our friends from above as there are proofs of crashed vehicles and wheat fields that have been patterned. Here's a bit of advice: when referring to them, always write or say "our friends from above". It's not even funny to do otherwise. One hundred and one rules for how to behave in the corporate workplace and one hundred and one hypotheses on how to teach a language. 10 rules on how to refer to Them. Do the math.

Simplicity is always the answer we are looking for.

Sightings, governmental conspiracy theorem, cover-ups, visitations, etcetera. No one really talks of how a long time ago they had been with us, cohabiting our reality. Except late night radio shows on AM. There are mentions of craft in the Bible. Woodcuts, in Renaissance paintings. They could be our beginning and ancestry. One day we'll figure out what planet we come from (the true mission of NASA). The previous parenthetical will be black markered out.

That's where the unidentified aspect of everything comes in. Just as we can really never know who our great great great grandparents were, we don't actually see these things darting about like steel cigars in the sky, behind clouds of mountains. I maintain I saw what I saw and it was the only valid form of epiphany that's worth discussing.

Really the discs that float above forests in Switzerland, or in the distance between telephone lines in a cornfield of Nebraska, or the balls of light that flew in the skies of a warm Phoenix evening, or the glowing donuts that appear in infrared films shot by the space shuttle crew are all just memories of the great exodus that hasn't ever been written down in the various arrays of bibles wild-eyed preachers are ready to quote from on Sunday morning low-budget t.v. shows.

The true indication that they exist is in the here and now. The evidence is in the way we cannot communicate with one another because we can't ever document the origins, the virgin birth of the big bang, if one will, of our collective, for lack of a better word, spawning. It is that long awkward silence. We cannot celebrate the beginning. We are not allowed to.

Take for instance my recent boss, of a long line of bosses bred specifically to be of the boss race. Randall, as he called himself, was the kind of guy who could simply never find a suit coat that fitted him properly. He was the type whose consciousness was forever itself hovering between what was real and the clever forces that paint the skies interesting. Sure, he could seem like he cared about the stresses and angst of students caught in between cultures in his center for "higher" learning, but he only had two temperaments: mellow and mellower.

No one remarked how obvious his iris-less eyes were because

everyone became instantly lost in his toothy grin and well-meaning demeanor. For him, every crisis about grading or student housing or the teachers' inability to make classes more fun than a New York Times crossword was met with the assumption that everything would turn out, somehow, "okay". Of course, it had to be o.k. Everything would be copasetic until the day giant discs appeared over the world's biggest cities and he could assume his true role: commander of the ultimate exchange program once dreamed up and fabulized as Soylent Green.

As I write this, the sky above the high desert lacks even one cloud. They know I'm at work on a heretical tract. They will only strike when and if I can get this published in a small printed collation read mostly by the loving mothers of the writers it features: a small press literary magazine. Those are even dying. It's part of the mega-plan. The last samizdat forum of individuality first slowly, now rapidly, being phased out. They will be in charge of the dreaming when it is time. The one collective dream.

Don't think I haven't been preparing for such a moment. The truck is gassed up. The guns are hidden, taped up under the seat. If these are my final last words, it can be assured that I'm not giving up without a fight.

The reason for this is that I'm not one of them. Somehow, I slipped through the cracks. I know they can feel me sweat when I see the orbs receding, bobbing over the tops of the asparagus-topped juniper trees, flecking into the horizon on badly moonlit nights. And I'll stand my ground being the proud Neanderthal that I am– the last one who believes in animal fantasies of love, friendship, and freethinking. Venues full of truth that no one reads about or thinks of anymore. Not when the wi-fi is on.

They cannot eradicate the ape in me.

And this is the reason why I cannot any longer hold a real job. Jobs are known to them as "perceptive servitude". This will be made clear by a tangential story. At the front of the English teaching school was Randall's henchman, a guy anonymously named Bill and he had the ability to see right through me. He had the training. He was bred as a seer.

With paper-thin spectacles, he tried to hide his own pupil-less eyes. When he spoke, his voice trembled in fear because he knew he was hiring a teacher with writerly pretensions, and as most know, writers equal danger.

One curious thing is that our friends from above don't even have an alphabet. All communication is telepathic or carried out through subtle hand gestures, barely perceptible to the human animal who relies on the much more vulgar form of body language.

Further proof: Bill's desk was chaos personified. He, perhaps, didn't want to signal that he was one of them by possessing an organized, sleek workspace. As he could see through anyone, anyone could see through him. Charts, tables, grade percentages, spreadsheets were all his obsessions. The trembling of his voice revealed his uneasiness with being the one appointed with the duty of controlling the façade of a language school.

He left his office only to enforce his rigid, rule following will on instructors. This he did through an endless array of nitpicking questions. He constantly quoted the objectives of learning and the need for grammar, and in doing this, in playing it real uncool, he blew his cover. He also smelled like dollar store lotion.

From the handbook: "Teach students the vocabulary of the body by singing the Hokey-Poky song".

Where in the world could they have gotten this from? Come on, only an alien would let this slip.

"Epiphanization" is my term for the moment a human sees through all the crap, the falseness, and the plastic guises they have put up and understands what is going on, what has been going on for ages. It doesn't happen to many. It'll happen to you, but when it does, you'd better run.

These days, I don't even bother to look up anymore. The sky is full of little silver twinkling things. It's more and more obvious and if you really spend an afternoon watching, you can tell they're getting bolder.

Just switch on the evening news. It's all right there, broadcast on such a low band that people are getting immune to the subtexts. The news is now a commercial for them and what they want us to be.

There's even a ring tone for it! It's pure B movie stuff. How stupid do they think we are? How stupid do they think some of us are?

Desolate, jagged, harsh, knife-blade-like mountains shaped and torn like an old cloth writhe to the end of perceptible distance. Like fences in all directions that don't hold anything back, the mountains surround and change colors from a greenish, gray tint to a low burning orange in the day's heat. A Martian resort whose background turns deep purple when it's about to rain. Tucked in the high altitude crevices and folds are pine and spruce trees, scared aspens, and a lot of juniper that covers hills and stretches into sage benches of abandoned fields, all a-tilt. This is the maniacal landscape that reminds them most of home.

Some crazies have put up a silhouette of Bigfoot because there is something about the grand nothingness that beckons primal thoughts. It's why they came here. It's the perfect place to establish a colony. No one would think to look here. Idaho. This state with a made up name is the personification of a weirdness they just adore. Most people can't even distinguish Idaho from Iowa anyway. It's what paradise turns into when it's made out of pure hell.

The phone is currently ringing. I will not answer it. Fuck, I just quit my job so that means I'm not taking any calls. I did it via e-mail.

I am not giving them a chance to touch me.

I know who it is anyway. It's probably my students wondering where I am. How I could disappear like that. I'll have to just let them wonder. It's really too late for them.

Or, it's the guys from the language school. They'll want to have a meeting I will never grant them. They'll want to talk about "what went wrong". They'll try to get me to see things from their point of view. They'll have objective sheets and brochures and suggestions. They will talk to me smiling. Their eyes will never blink. It has been eighteen rings until it the phone finally mutes itself. No normal human lets a phone ring for eighteen rings. Unless they're just about to murder.

Finally, the high desert brings rain. Behind the storm scuds ripped to shreds by the rounded pyramid of Pinpoint Mountain, I can hear a subtle hummm. I know the saucers are taking the opportunity of weather to deploy more of their kind. Horses whinny and that means they know too. I'm not as stupid as they think I am. And horses are never wrong.

The truck is gassed up. I'll get some ammo at Buck's. I'll get a case of cheap white wine. I've got my music. I've got a little time before the take over is complete. Just read the newspapers people. Study the newscasters' faces and watch them on the verge of flinching. It's happening everywhere. It's happening day by day. Watch the vapid t.v. shows and the clues are there. No one talks about anything these days. It's all smiles and whatever, whatever, until they own you. Until you can't think anymore. There's only two places our kind has a chance.

Death. Or Canada.

boreal

RAISON D'ÊTRE

The beautiful couples will pass me by. How I love to look at the smiles on the men's faces. Their teeth shine anticipating liquor. I remember how I was once like them. The ones who think they are alone and have chosen not to be.

Her shoe is half-on, half-off her long, slender foot. Her legs are crossed and her toe points towards the streets full of people who walk with their arms entwined, their mouths open. They are talking of yesterdays. Back when there was a time to roam the alleys of the city and squint at cracked street lamps. Between the wars. Wine flowed in rivulets, spilling from tabletops into streams down the sewer. The cantonnier's rags were soaked in it, looking like mangled birds. The rats, for a while, slept full and were contentedly drunk.

The consensus was that when it stormed, life was drizzled on for a purpose. Rainy, grey days left the populace with an aftertaste of sorrow, or empathy. People sat under the dripping awnings not to eat. They talked. In rooms in apartment buildings above first floors, children's cries were muffled by lamp shades. A single gunshot could be deciphered almost near dusk.

Many have jotted down details such as these. Many eat in the best and worst restaurants. *The Grind. The Broom Closet. The Hereafter.* We have all been with more men and women than either of us care to remember. Later, when evening closes its black umbrella, we walk nearly the same leafless streets. If I see her, I will turn away, not knowing whose hair is wound with hers. I will not glance at her soap-white forehead. I will not acknowledge the tiredness in my own legs or the remorse etched into the wrinkles of my watchband. That night I will find myself alone in the park.

The beautiful couples will pass me by. How I love to look at the smiles on the men's faces. Their teeth shine anticipating liquor. I remember how I was once like them. The ones who think they are alone and have chosen not to be.

A PROPER BURIAL

It was too cold to bury anything. The second week of February and the ground was frozen solid. Funny how the little street was in the process of breaking itself apart. It bee-lined across the ugly part of the town and was used as a short-cut to skirt the main road's traffic. Riddled with more than just potholes, whole sections of it were coming unbuckled and sinking sometimes half of a foot. Hardly any cars anymore dared to risk the few minutes of time it would save to the next stoplight, which would invariably be red. Leaves of last autumn still clogged its gutters with trash that shared a similar dirty brown color. The abandoned house on the hill that overlooked it clearly billboarded the words Keep Out.

There on the lawn under the bare branches of the elm tree it lay. A dead squirrel. It still looked alive, the bushy hair of its tail, its coat of fur, moving in the wind. Except for the tag of dark auburn around its head and swollen neck. The ground underneath so hard and solid.

We all had been aware of it. The drifts of snow had melted into dirty lumps of powder during a freak revival of spring. But winter had left its calling card in the plowed piles of white-pack and was here to keep the windows secured for months, painting them in an opaque mist of crystalline. But these were only excuses for not noticing.

Our bay window had evaded the gusts of wind and remained clear and as cold as a slab of ice. Icicles hung from above it like an ornamental fence spun from glass. Julie had an ability to tell the temperature by placing her hands on the window and blowing on it, making an oval of fog. She was the first to acknowledge the tragedy.

"So what are we going to do about it. The dead thing" she asked.

"What? Who died?" Taylor said.

"You guys know. The squirrel" she pointed beyond the abstraction of the lamp's glare on the window.

Taylor said he didn't know what she was talking about. I merely couldn't figure her melodramatics. It was only road kill. The three of us drove or biked by so many of them everyday. Because this small town, which wasn't really all that small anymore, still not exactly a city, had sprung up in the flood plain between two forested ridges, the animals of the surrounding woods had a hard time knowing where nature ended and where civilization began. It was one of those dubiously titled "Tree Cities". When viewed from above, on a dual engine shuttle to Minneapolis, the buildings looked like outcrops of stone among a blanket of brown, human monotony invading a Zen pasture. This winter was lasting so long that we were beginning to forget the concept of shade.

"Well, I guess he is sort of our collective pet, but can't we call the dog pound to come out and remove him?"

Julie read the logic of my argument but wanted more immediate action. She couldn't overlook the tragedy as easily as Taylor obviously did, she being the more introspective of the two. They had been married a year and eight months and the yin-yang aspect of their coupling was emphasizing itself at the moment.

"Couldn't we take care of it?"

"Yeah, sure," Taylor replied from the kitchen, "but not right now. I'm trying to make dinner."

"You mean something like put it in a plastic bag and leave it on the corner for the garbage men?"

"No, how gross! I don't know what exactly. Something better than that."

Julie stood in her light blue robe and moved the thermostat down a couple of notches. "I'm off to work," she spun around and ran up the staircase. It took her minutes to get dressed and leave. Even though the weather called for leather boots, warm socks and thick panty hose, she still painted her toenails red.

~

After eating the stew of vegetables Taylor made for dinner, we thought of how we could occupy our Saturday night. The house was warmed with the smell of cooking and most of the lamps were on. It was a compact little place: three rooms upstairs, two below, and there was even a lean-to garage. Pretty nice for the amount of rent we shared.

I was on my way out of this corner of the woods, having recently ended my schooling, and was trying to find work in any major metropolis that would have me. I had enough of the boondocks mainly because of the lack of opportunity that marginal cities connecting the major gathering places of the northern states offered. When my lease ran out, the only two friends in the world came though and let me move in for the time being.

And the time being means uncertainty. I figured that if my hundred fold applications for jobs didn't result in anything then I would move to the city of my choice. The northwest looked good, at least on maps. Then there is always California. I tried to do as much as I could, things like the dishes, work on their car, anything to help them get by. Julie worked as a secretary in the hospital. Taylor worked shifts at a data processing company. They met each other at a party after a jazz concert and fell in love under the rainy skies of summer two years ago. Their weird hours were putting a strain on their newlywed status, though neither would admit it.

Now there was this to do. Taylor was relaxing with a cigarette, his feet propped on the couch.

"Shall I take care of the matter at hand or do you want to help me with the honors?" I asked him.

"Give me a few minutes, and we'll both go out." He put his cigarette down to dust off an album and place it gently on the turntable.

As I laced up my boots, the sounds of saxophone and bass were driving from the speakers. Not exactly a dirge or Albinoni's adagio, but the mood of the night was struck. Taylor put on his long rancher coat and we went out into the cold air and streetlights of evening. With the wind chill, it was below zero.

The squirrel's body was acquiring a frost like a ruffled collar and its small dinosaur front paws were held out clutching nothing. Taylor stubbornly trodded to the garage and brought back a shovel. A car drove down the road illuminating his glasses, but not his eyes, in two quick flashes. He placed the tip of the blade next to the animal and jumped on the shovel's flat edge. It broke only centimeters into the ground.

"I guess you're right," he said, "but I had to test it. God, it's fucking cold!"

"Even though I told Julie I wouldn't, why don't I get a garbage bag, you shovel it in, and we go toss it somewhere?" I followed.

Taylor acknowledged my suggestion with a nod and tried throwing the shovel into the earth like one would a javelin.

"Okay, okay. Hurry, I'm freezing."

When I came back, he was balancing the stiff body on the shovel's blade. I opened the mouth of the bag and he placed it in cautiously.

"Stick it in the car and we'll find somewhere to dispose of it. The thing's heavy as a brick" Taylor quipped with the keys jingling in his pocket as he made for the car. I got in the passenger's side and put the bag on the floor behind me.

"If this happens again in the summer, Julie will have to deal with the rotting meat," he said while hitting the ignition.

We headed out into the darkness. Neither of us were sure where to go. A garbage bin behind the supermarket would do the trick and I reminded Taylor that it was as far as we'd have to go. Toss it in the dumpster and let the someone else deal with it. The city was responsible for the death anyway. As we were following the other main road, I saw a turn-off leading south of town. I had never taken this road. Thirty feet before we approached it, I yelled, "Turn here!"

"Okay, but where the hell are you taking us? This leads to that ghost town of a place, Creek Junction. Beyond that, there's a quarry and then nothing."

"Then it's to the quarry."

Not much of the landscape could be seen. It was a night without a moon and clear skies overhead. I thought I saw the constellation Leo but the road turned so many times I could only keep its tail in view. We could see up the length of the hills dotted in pine and mostly hardwood trees grown wild. Even though it was winter, the dried grasses still stood at chest-level. Sometimes the lights of a farmhouse appeared on the hills and we could see the silhouettes of the windows' crosses. There was nothing else.

About fifteen miles down, we saw a sign for the quarry, but when we pulled up to its dirt road, there was a fence securely chained with shining new masterlocks.

"There goes that," Taylor said. "I'm not getting arrested for trespassing."

"Yeah, so let's drive a little farther. We're in the country now. There might be a roadside park or something up ahead."

"There is something up ahead. It's called the Deep South."

"Just for a few miles. I've never been this way."

So we continued. Taking corners at forty made the bag slide around in the back. We both winced at the sound.

When we came around a bend and saw the sign for Coon's Marsh, we thought we had found the place. The red arrow pointed down a gravel stretch that led down a hill. With the brights on, we could tell the road soon swerved.

Taylor took the turn and continued his speed leaving a rooster tail of white dust behind. The gravel taking us nowhere was filled with sinkholes and the ride was getting real bumpy like a graded mountain road. We were starting to wonder about this.

I could see the lights reflecting off of a shiny surface yards in the distance. When Taylor slowed down for a major rut, I saw pieces of ice floating down a liquid surface. It was the river. Taylor continued slowly, then stopped all together and said, "check that out–"

He positioned the car so the headlights shone on a length of barbed wire fence fastened to rotting poles of wood. Tall yellow grass was growing through the fence and we could make out white monoliths of stone behind. Barely visible, a string of wire had been manipulated into the word Beauchamp within the matrix of the fence. It was a long forgotten cemetery.

"Perfect. Just perfect," he said.

We got out of the car. Taylor found a flashlight in the glove box and I picked up the garbage bag by its neck and held it an arm's length. We hopped the fence and Taylor, way ahead of me, was inspecting the tombstones that stood nearly two feet high.

"This one's from 1879. There's a relief of a dove on it. Pretty weird."

I stood by his side and looked at the ancient marker. The one next to it had a hand pointing upwards. A last hopeful gesture. The few trees left on the outskirts of the plain were creaking in the wind. There were no flowers at the base of the tombstones. No trace of humans. Probably no one had been here for years.

"I guess people from the city still have some relatives out here," I said.

"Might be so, but how would they know. This place is probably closed. Hey, how about that, a cemetery without a waiting list?"

"Let's get rid of this before I catch some kind of disease from it. Who knows how long it's been dead. There could be a handful of maggots going at its insides."

The land sloped into a field of driftwood then riverbank. It was Taylor's idea to give it a burial at sea. So we walked toward the water with the spotlight of yellow at our feet. Soon the batteries would be drained and there could be raccoons out this late. At the river, I held on to the bottom of the bag and the squirrel rolled out into the water with a loud plunk. Taylor hummed taps under his breath. Branches were breaking the surface and pointing like gnarled arrows downstream.

We crossed the cemetery checking out every other gravestone. Some were decorated with writing too eroded to read. A few of the stones were toppled over due to the swell of the land and a couple of them were broken in two, the rain staining them black and the earth and vegetation surrounding eager to swallow them up. Ashes to ashes, dust to dust? More like bone to ground, bone to ground.

~

That night in bed, I heard Julie come home. I couldn't fall asleep so I was listening to a talk radio station turned down real low while I was studying the patterns of whiteness the streetlights spilled onto my ceiling. Their bedroom was down the hall from mine but the hardwood floors and walls transmitted sounds every so often. The wind had to be blowing right.

I heard Julie and Taylor talking for a while. It sounded like it might have been an argument, but they were trying to keep it down. After I heard the click of the light turning off and the bed springs sounding like hungry birds, I covered my head with the blanket and tried and tried to go to sleep.

~

Sunday morning. Julie woke me up by playing the stereo much too loud but what could I say, I was a guest in the house. Taylor was in the kitchen finishing the breakfast he made for himself, then was off to work. He called up the stairs, "You'll have to fend for yourselves, I gotta go. Why don't you take a morning drive in the country and show Julie what we were up to last night?"

I said, "As soon as I'm awake." It was 9:30 a.m.

The first question she asked me as I slid down the stairs was if we had gone to a bar last night. I told her, "No." It was what Taylor told me to say if she asked. He had explained to me what her stance on bars was. "She thinks they're meat markets, and the only reason guys go to them is to find women," I remember him saying months ago. When we went it was mainly out of boredom and to blow the steam off the dull rituals of everyday life. I talked most of the time trying to verbalize the plans for the future that were still ambiguous in my head and Taylor drank. Julie was before me now. I didn't like telling her anything about us. It's a most dangerous game to become a married man or woman's confidant. Especially when you start telling him or her lies.

"So where are we going?" she asked.

"It'll be easier for me to show you rather than explain. That is, if I can find it."

She looked at me puzzled.

The drive there in the daylight took a lot of the mystery out of the trip. We saw the shanties with garbage, abandoned cars, a few dogs, and toys strewn among their yards and the couple of gothic farm houses restored to a livable condition. We passed the craters filled with bright blue water at the quarry. If we had crossed the fence there last night, surely we would have been swimming at some point.

I found the gravel road and navigated its winding path. It was much more tame in the day. Julie asked, "Where the hell are we going?" while holding onto the shoulder strap of her seat belt.

"Just over here," I pointed.

She didn't say a word when she saw our destination.

I helped her over the fence and we walked through the rows of tombstones and grave markers. The river looked like it was at the point of overflowing, swelling at its banks only a hundred yards away. At some of the markers, there actually were shriveled up bouquets of flowers and sun-bleached American flags.

"These are the kind of graves you put paper over and get an impression from with a charcoal pencil," she said.

"Pretty amazing, huh?"

"So this is what you two did last night. How did you ever find it?"

"Oh, I'd known about it. Guess I read about it in the paper or something. Come here, look at this one."

At that moment, I found a tombstone that was unlike any other there. It was waist-high and chipped away at the edges, dated 1892-1894. A child was buried beneath. That's probably why it had the impression of a squirrel holding an acorn. I had never seen anything like it.

"We put him in the river, but if the ground could have been broken, this is where he would have gone," I said patting the stone with the flat of my palm.

Julie smiled. With wide-open eyes she bent down to examine the dates. She couldn't help feeling the relief of the stone animal and tracing the inscription with her fingers. When she stood up, it looked like she had tears forming in the corners of her eyes.

She said, "It's so beautiful here." I took her hand in mine, it was so cold out. She looked back once more as we walked back to the car, stopped our return, and kissed me, the tip of her nose frozen, on my cheek.

AT 8,000 FEET

It hasn't snowed for weeks, but the low temperature up here in the mountains has kept them white, and that's our main concern. Dana, for the first time I think, realized how big the city actually was on our way up when we stopped our ascent to piss behind the hardened drifts the plows made to clear the treacherous path through the foothills. She said she could see where the city stopped, the wheat-colored beach, then the monotone of ocean. What she really was fixating upon was a cloudbank caught in a valley drowning the outskirts of the metropolis, not even the great city itself. But I wasn't about to sour her vision of tranquility. Just wait until we were to return down the slope at night and Los Angeles, with its power plants and airstrips, would be lit up like an unending carnival. What would she see then?

We decided on a decent place to stay— a sort of Hollywood style pseudo-lodge, more of a pine-paneled motel—but at least it had all the comforts of home, including a fireplace. This trip wasn't exactly well-planned between the five of us. We desperately had wanted to get out of the daily routine of downtown, beach, highway, work, restaurant, and so headed for these snow-capped peaks the day after an ocean wind blew the smog from the valley and we could finally see what had been surrounding us all this time. Since Caroline and I were only visiting, we'd never had the chance to view the city as the cul-de-sac it was, bordered wildly by so much water and land. On that clear day before we left, I cornered the hill that separates the suburbs from the beach communities, looked in the rearview, and thought I was leaving Pakistan. Blue mountains stationary under a blue sky.

Dana and Mark were veteran skiers, according to Dana; her husband wasn't one too much for words. He seemed at peace behind the wheel, occasionally glancing at the buildings and warehouses which had begun to thin out the farther we followed the three, then two lane highway. After we passed the final truck stop and crossed the gas station and quick shop badlands of the smaller sub-cities, it was an icy one-way path that led straight to the mountaintop and the barren stretch of desert behind. Mark would scan up and down the radio dial to find the exact song that would complement his exact mood at the exact moment, sometimes checking the rearview to see if we were bored or annoyed by the change of atmosphere from jazz to pop to classical.

Caroline was well into her book and my son, Alex, was nodding off. I was enjoying the mere fact of travel, the change of scenery, and leaving the gridlock that normally kept my roving curiosity occupied. This would be Alex's first time on the slopes. It was only my second time although I was sure I would be able to gracefully glide down the incline as soon as I reached the top. It looks so easy on television. Caroline wasn't so cocksure, she was even a little nervously excited, imbued with only a memory of trying the sport as a child growing up in western Canada.

A seemingly endless queue of cars and off-road vehicles had formed on the highway into the hill town so we decided to find our cabin, gear up, and head out. After driving up and down the pine -ridged drag a couple of times, we found our place nestled in a stand of trees and dirty snow banks.

Dana wanted to hit the mountain before the crowds so we ventured out to eat breakfast. We found a place up the road, an eatery in a cabin that was decorated with photographs of movie and television stars that frequented the area. Well, those who at least stopped by once. I even thought I recognized a minor star sitting at a table with a very attractive woman. Strange to see an image from the screen in the flesh. He looked the same as he did in the moving pictures, although a little more leathery.

After we got our skis and suited up, Alex became upset at our decision to enroll him in a class. He told me, making sure that everyone else would hear, that if his real mom were here, she would let him have at the bunny slope at least. Maybe he was right and I was being overly cautious, but since I was ordained by law to have only these limited periods of vacation time with him, I couldn't risk flying him home in a body cast. I tried to explain this but he just stared down into thousands of footprints in the snow. I wondered why even the mountains couldn't alleviate the ongoing hassle of my previous marriage and a past that I thought the both of us wanted, at least for a time, to leave behind.

"He'll get over it. It'll only be for an hour and a half," Caroline assured. We left him with a ski instructor who had his name, *Rayzer*, stitched to his jacket.

~

On the lift up to the double diamond slope, Caroline and I were silent. She was turned around looking at the scenery behind us and deeply breathing in the cold air. I was measuring our elevating height and thinking how easy it would be to slip out underneath the bar and break my back on the outcropping of stone and spears of pines below. The sunlight was blinding.

Mark and Dana were on the lift in front of us, waving and saying something. Dana was pointing to her left and down the mountain. I turned to see what she was gesturing to, losing my already frayed sense of balance, almost dropping a pole. With my hands making a baseball bill over my eyes, I saw Alex at the bottom of the training hill, splayed like a hastily drawn X on a map.

They took off down the run with out hesitation, even though Mark was supposed to act as our instructor, so we awkwardly followed. Caroline began slowly, broadly sweeping a path from left to right. I took the more expedient route, nearly straight down into the crowds of yelling kids and right in the way of the streamlining veterans. It was true: the body's memory is at times more accurate than the brain's. My knees bent, my torso leaned into the turns. It was like riding a bicycle after years of not being near one. I had a pair of two-foot long plastic skis as a kid. It was all coming back to me. Time eroding in a white blur of snow, cold air, descending.

Midway down, I slowed to let Caroline catch up. When she did and motioned for me to continue, I let off with reckless abandon. The snow was more ice; I could hear the edges of my skis cutting into it like a diamond into glass. My speed was increasing by the second but I couldn't feel it. I could only hear the wind. I headed straight for the center of a drop and encountered a ridge that lead to another trail, one with no skiers, no people, nobody—this was my last thought. I must have been doing fifty when I hit the mogul, took flight, and did my impression of that skier in the Olympics just as the voice-over solemnly intones *the agony of defeat.* The pain was unbearable once my body stopped spinning. The snow in my clothes, down my back, around my wrists, was burning. I had lost a ski with an accompanying throb in my knee. My lip was bleeding. The moment was glorious.

Caroline found me a few minutes later. I could tell she was concerned but was also repressing one hell of a smile. I was laughing, although it sounded more like a wail. She had retrieved my ski which I was barely able to clip back on and I followed her down to the bottom.

"You two get lost up there?" Dana asked as we cruised into the next lift area. Mark was grinning wildly.

"That's what it's all about," he said. "Getting to know the mountain intimately."

~

I was still shaking when I met Alex, who too had snow stuck to his jacket, especially around the collar. He was over his anger and anxious to follow my lead.

"Don't worry Dad, kids' bones are like rubber, I'm not going to break anything."

"You're probably right, just take your time. I'll be right behind you."

We caught the lift after a long, silent wait. I noticed that the lines were peopled with the very attractive type. Some of the women were wearing such fashionable ski-wear that they looked more apt to ballroom waltz down the slopes. The men were intense and vocal, intent on conquering every run before the four thirty call.

Alex watched the others speed under us on our chair ride up. I thought I saw Dana and Mark getting off the adjacent lift. I lost a glove in my crash and my hand was becoming blue with the cold. The clement, cold weather at the base had hardened into the arctic of the peak. The day was good and the snow couldn't be finer. Dana couldn't help herself any longer. She chided Mark into following her to the triple and quadruple diamond runs. We didn't mind their absence. Caroline, Alex, and I were having a time on the more mediocre runs– racing each other, attempting jumps and skirting up the steep embankments, and about every half hour, colliding in a tangle of skis and laughter.

Near four, we all met at the lodge and decided to find somewhere to get some food. We were famished and sore. It was quitting time.

In the parking lot, we de-suited and stupidly left our gear in the back of the jeep. The next day, we would wake to find our clothes and boots frozen together and painfully cold. We learned that experience was an acquired taste. We weren't thinking that far ahead into the future. The image of a fireplace burning with its plastic logs was all I could immediately picture. Mark had brought along a case of beer. Dana had her pack of smokes; Caroline and Alex brought some books to read together and I had absolutely nothing to do. No office work, no plans to implement, no matters that needed my attention. We turned the t.v. on and kicked back waiting for the pizza to be delivered. We all even agreed on the toppings.

Mark was sipping his third beer and flipping through the channels when he motioned to me and said, "Hey, check this out!"

The screen showed the downtown streets lit by a few streetlights, the throbbing red of the police lighting up the fronds of the surrounding palms. A tense voice-over spoke a narrative of dread and urgency:

'At seven tonight, the assailants realized the attempted robbery could not be pulled off due to the employee's setting off the alarm. The police came onto the scene shortly after. One woman escaped before they could take her hostage. She has told us that four men rounded up the people in the bank. Our reports tell us now that there is only one person holding the others hostage. It is thought that three others are masquerading as hostages. More as these events unfold.'

We were riveted. This was exactly why I wanted to get away from the city. Now I was back down there, electrified by the fray.

Then the telephone rang. It was Alex's mother. She needed to talk to me. She wanted him to be home in two days, which meant we would have to leave the next morning. I told her it was really impossible, but she wouldn't listen. I didn't even think how she got the number. On the screen, there were men approaching the bank. A figure inside behind the glass doors was waving them away.

Alex wanted to talk to his mom. I told him to try to convince her into letting him stay for a few extra days.

"Tell her you're beginning to get sick or something. Just three more days. We're far from home."

Alex winced. He stared into the fire, his eyes straying to the television, then back to the fire.

'It seems that as a gesture of goodwill or bargaining, the hostage-takers are letting some of the people go,' the voice said. A line of five people at first slowly exited the bank. Once they were fifty feet outside they ran towards the ambulances and were immediately, almost violently, taken in by the police. Among them could be one of the perpetrators.

I got back on the phone with my ex-wife, Linda, and I could tell she was resolute in ruining our attempt at a vacation. Her voice was quavering. She would be contacting her lawyer if the boy wasn't home the day after the next. The few beers I had drunk fueled my anger and I let loose. The past and my infidelities was all she really wanted to talk about. The past followed me wherever I went. There was no escaping it, no reprieve from it not even for one weekend.

At almost the instant I began to yell, Alex began to cry. Tears were falling on the slice of pizza he was trying to eat. So I simply hung up.

The police in a dark, crouching band approached the one large sheet glass window of the bank from either side of its view. The screen filled with a lightening-like explosion, then a cloud of white. A man inside ran through the smoke waving his arms above his head. There looked like there was a long, skinny object in his right hand. He ran straight into two of the crouching officers, who were beginning to stand, and at mid-movement, then emptied their revolvers into his chest. The man fell into a clenched position and the rest of the force charged the bank. Through the disseminating fog, screams of those inside were clearly heard. A mass of bodies laying on their stomachs, splayed out upon the floor like babes in a maternity ward. Fear had released them.

Dana wanted to know what the phone call was about. Caroline, by means of a learned telepathy, knew. I told her, "The usual." Later in the evening, Mark told me that I shouldn't raise my voice, that it didn't help matters any. I knew he could be right, but what did he really know? Caroline was finished eating and was reading with Alex: a book of World Geography. She asked us if we could turn the t.v. off.

I went outside with Dana to have a cigarette. The air was crisp. She apologized for bringing us up here. She said she only wanted the opportunity to bring us all together. I told her it wasn't her fault. There was a gradual mist beginning to form in the sharp air. It looked steely blue against the snow. The lights of the city shimmered miles in the distance. Across the road, a ski run was lit up for the night. There was no one on the hill. Only the swerving ski trails of the day remained like fingernail traces after sex. By tomorrow morning, snow machines would obliterate them and the events of the day in mountains and cities of the world, invisible.

OUR LADY OF THE GUARD

You see them wherever you go. On Broome Street, Sunday mornings, walking arm in arm. He wears a trench coat and carries a Times under his elbow. She's telling him something private and unimportant and hanging onto a leash that harnesses a non-descript mutt. The dog sniffs at every other wad of garbage and stain on the sidewalk. All three are oblivious to the steady drizzle and bare branches of the maples holding down the sidewalks at catty-corner. Or they're on Michigan Avenue drinking steaming cups of coffee out of wax-coated paper cups, smiling and walking slowly over the bridge and looking through its eroding segments to see the green river at standstill. In an early afternoon dusting of snow, they're silent thinking each other's thoughts. Come evening, they're at the beach after sunset. Theirs is the only car in the empty parking lot that has become a gathering point for hungry seagulls. A flick of a lighter illuminates the moving silhouettes of their heads for an instant. Voices from the radio slip out of the window cracked open. The surf churns up foam, empty bottles, cigarette butts, and strands of seaweed on the white stones blackened at their base where they touch water.

The traffic is heavy at this time of night. I wait impatiently on the roadside ready to jaywalk. Soon the soccer stadium will be filling with rowdy coliseum goers. Already, some are racing from their neighborhood bars to get the best parking and seats available. It's obvious who they are not only by the speed at which they're driving these winding streets, but by the local team's song they honk out as they pass the beach-side restaurants. *Doot dadoot doot doot doot.*

Because it's winter, the city isn't as crowed as it normally is and that's why I'm out walking tonight. There's a certain edifying solitude in being in prime locations at the wrong time. The almost abandoned bars in skiing towns during long American summers. The barren streets of Phoenix in the searing afternoon sun. Or Los Angeles whenever it rains.

The statue the city has erected at its main intersection points eastwards and gives me my cue. I have an hour to make it up the hill to the cathedral. In my backpack I have all I need for my pilgrimage: a notebook and a bottle of water. The hillside dwellings are painted a salmon color of orange. The adobe walls that attempt to conceal them are lined with pieces of broken bottles of varying hues: green, blue, lacquer brown. I carefully put my hand over one of the points to find that it has been dulled by erosion. The leveling power of the wind is a force in these parts.

The hill's seemingly innocuous elevation of two hundred or so meters has me breathing hard three-quarters of the way up. This terrain, which is semi-arid, has formed steep outcroppings of calcite on which the city clings. The landscape is more like desert than temperate zone, but it's is well-concealed by pines that spring from anywhere the dusty soil has gathered. There's a garden of wild vegetation bounded by yuccas. It's hard not to continue up the path without looking towards Golgotha. I pass a woman in a fur coat carrying a bag of oranges and she says something about the wonderful view that awaits me. Her hair is dyed with henna and she descends the hill in high heels.

The Moorish spires of the cathedral reach into a blinding sky. On them are black stains of gunfire that the Germans left when they attempted to take the citadel. As a matter of pride, the locals let it be known that this part of the country has never been under a Teutonic yoke. Every crack and fissure of the edifice highlighted by a dark erosive effect of rainwater which emphasizes its age and longevity. From a distance, it looks like the walls are growing hair.

When I reached the hilltop, it was surprising to see a group of older Arabs as the only visitors. The men dressed in grey jackets with their white chechias. The women in resplendent djellabas lined in gold lamé, walking up the stairs slowly because of their swollen ankles. When they reached the top piazza, myself steps behind, they looked at the sea and pointed out towards the clouds where Algeria might be. Or Morocco. Perhaps Tunisia. An Egyptian ocean liner steadily crosses the water in-between the islands of the bay. It was from the great height that the labyrinth of the city became apparent. The tight matrix of red-tiled, concrete buildings below us was beginning to make sense.

There was a couple on the highest view point holding each other and speaking quietly. They were unaware of the futility of traffic and the ships bellowing their horns as they slowly maneuvered into port. The two were awaiting what was theirs that evening– the sun falling into the sea.

Once I entered the cathedral, I no longer wondered why believers of another faith would be touring this temple. The singing of monks piped in on tiny, modern, concealed speakers added to the liminal effect. The ornate interior diffused such a small irony.

It was more of an art gallery: there were paintings hung on the wall, mobiles of wooden ships strung from the vaulted ceiling, and mosaics of the most stunning colors looking down at a few quiet meditators. The paintings, from what I could make out, were done by locals who had been in some perilous circumstance and, with the grace of divine intervention, survived to tell their stories. Some were done by children. There was a painting of a downed Sopwith Camel with its pilot lying dazed over the target symbol on the wing and a radiant virgin watching over the scene. Heaven in the upper right hand corner.

Another was of a cat flung to the side of the road by a car, yet miraculously alive, the red tag of its tongue sticking out. There were paintings of clipper ships on stormy seas; of bus crashes in the country; invalids with smiling faces in the hospital. All had the virgin looking over them arrayed in colors of glory.

The whispering of a barely audible voice brought me back from my momentary trance. A little, bent-over woman in the front pews garnered my attention. She was busy saying the rosary. When I saw the babushka covering her head, I knew who it was. I even knew her name. Angèle.

I am a long unknown relative of hers– her sister's grandson– and I had found her name in the address book of my grandmother's years ago. I called her just two days ago and explained as best I could who I was, and since I was in this part of the country, I would like to meet her. It was a mystery why someone related to me might be in a country so far from the wilds of Northeast Europe from where the legacy of my line had come. She agreed to my visit and was now patiently awaiting my arrival steeped in a faith I didn't share.

"Hello Madame, let me introduce myself..." I began. She said my name and embraced me.

"You are the spitting image of your mother. It is so good to finally meet you."

I helped her up and offered to take her to lunch in the cafeteria nearby but she refused and told me that we would have lunch at her place not too far from here.

On the bus ride to her house, she pointed out to me the houses of neighbors and people she knew. There was the mansion of a Christian Lebanese general who is seeking asylum in the city. The relatively ornate house was guarded by militia men and was severed from the streets by heavy, moveable iron barricades. It leaned on a crag at the sea's edge. There was the apartment of Edward who lost his arm in the war and who came over on Thursday nights to drink whiskey and play cards. There is where Lorraine lived with her three sisters, all who cooked meals for the nuns in the Orthodox convent. Angèle gave the city that kept to itself behind bright green shutters and blue-tiled addresses a personality.

Her house was a tiny affair that was really more garden than living quarters. She apologized for it being winter hence the absence of the carnations and gladiolas that regularly surrounded the place. Inside I was greeted by her son, decades older than I, and a lethargic black cat named Fishbone.

She made her son, Aldo, and me some soup as if we both were regular visitors who came daily for lunch, while she tinkered around the kitchen and sang a tune under her breath. Aldo was amazed by my presence and asked me many questions. We ate our meal and told our stories between mouthfuls of soup, then bread, then fish, then salad, then cakes. When the food finally stopped, she sat down next to me and simply smiled. I asked her how she got here and why. She began by saying, "Oh, that old story, well, all right ...."

'When I was a little girl, about fifteen or sixteen, I worked on a farm. I was in charge of the daily chores, you know, watering the chickens and the ducks, taking hay to the cows, collecting eggs, feeding the goats, combing the horses manes. There was another worker there named Gregor who was of the marrying age and who was, although I didn't know it at the time, seeking me as his prospect. He wasn't an ugly man but he was large and burly and he had lost an eye when a stubborn mule decided to kick him in the head rather than move.

'One day this Gregor with one eye wanted to help me get the hay for the cows. I can remember the day because it had been raining like the dickens for three days, and this day the rain was sparse, like a mist. The thunderheads were rumbling in the distance but the wind was pushing them away from our neck of the woods and the skies were a lighter grey than they had been. It almost looked like day in the daytime.

'Since he wanted to assist me, I let him because haying the cows was not very fun for me. Although I was a strong girl, the hay was scratchy, getting into my blouse and hair, and heavier than you think. He followed me up the ladder to the loft where the hay was stored. We began pushing clumps of it off the loft to the floor and sweating like pigs because it is much warmer at the top of the barn than at the bottom where there are doors. He took off his shirt while I had to stop every few minutes to wipe the sweat from my brows and eyes. I joked with him saying that it must be easier for him to work hard because the sweat could only go into one of his eyes so he shouldn't have to stop as often as I.

'When I turned to acknowledge my bit of humor, I saw him standing there looking at me. Then he quite mechanically pulled at the rope that held his burlap pants on his waist, and let me say, he did not look tired at all. His ... his ... his thing was straight up like the handle of a pitchfork, of which I first thought it was, and he took me by the arms, breathing like an animal, and threw me into the bundle of hay. I was a young girl and didn't know what was going to happen, although I had an idea of what was taking place.

'Once father had told me to throw ice cold water from the trough on the stray dog who got stuck in a barn cat when I found them both wailing together in the grain house.

'Gregor had much the very same look in his eye as that poor old dog did.

'I said no, no Gregor, don't treat me like an animal of the barn. You can do whatever you like but please go get a blanket, even if it is the old blanket we put under the horse's saddle. The hay and sharp pieces of straw may cut me so and father will ask me about the cuts when I bathe myself in the tub tonight.

'He held me so close that the sweat from his forehead dropped into my eyes, burning my sight. Everything became blurry. He looked at me so deeply that I thought he had passed out with his one good eye open, but I could hear his breath and his tongue stopping in the back of his throat like an arrow being held on a bow about to be unleashed from its quiver.

After his moment of thought, he agreed but was unable to retie the knot of rope fastened to his pants, so let them fall to his ankles and hobbled down the ladder. He took the blanket from a peg on the wall and hopped up the ladder without even using his hands.

'When he was almost to the loft, with my bare feet I pushed the ladder as far out as I could. Gregor then grabbed it with his hands and, on the ladder, stood straight up and down.

With much exertion, he managed to balance on the ladder, I thought that it might fall back onto the loft and I would be raped, maybe become pregnant, and have to marry this awful man and this terrible future played out like a moving picture in my mind. But when his pants tore in half from between his ankles and he looked down, the ladder toppled backwards and he fell to the ground on his back.

'I yelled for help and Poppa came into the barn. I said that Gregor fell because I accidentally pushed the ladder away from the loft with a stroke of the pitchfork. Gregor was moaning—lying in the dirt with the rags of his pants around his ankles and we never discussed the event ever again.

'It turned out that Gregor had only broken his shoulder bone and some ribs and would return to our farm in the fall when he was better. I knew that something terrible would happen to me if we were both to be working in a field beyond a call to the house. Then I knew I had to leave.

'Your Grandmother had saved enough money to take the boat to America and before she left, she gave me the name of a family living in Paris who had posted a work notice at the University. These people needed a maid to keep the house and care for the children so I wrote them a letter and they offered me the job.

'So I was off to Paris. It was a much better life. I lived in a big house and would only have to go to the street to find milk and the finest cheeses and bread, and good bread at that. The man I worked for was a government official and paid me well and the children were darling and I was very happy. Then the Germans came and took the city and the family I worked for had to leave. Without an explanation, they told me I should get out of the city and go far away to be safe. They were moving to another country, but they wouldn't tell me where to ensure my own safety. I packed what little I had, and with a friend of mine who was a cook in a restaurant that the Germans shut down, went to the government office to find work somewhere else.

At this point, Angèle's speech began to wax more and more into an accent and it became harder for me to understand her story. Aldo helped me out by translating phrases here and there. I noticed her eyes began to gloss over with a wetness as she spoke staring at an embroidered pattern on the table cloth.

It so happened that the Germans briefly were in control of the hospital here in the southern part of the country. When they left, the Italians took over but soon abandoned it as the war changed to different theaters, and so for reasons beyond my knowledge, the British took control. We were offered jobs doing the laundry and whatnot but we had to hitchhike down here from Paris. In between Paris and here, a farmer dropped us off in a city, I can't remember the name, but it was large enough to have a zoo, and because he knew someone who worked there, he suggested that we stay there until he could arrange a ride for us to reach the hospital.

'We used the cloth bags that carried what little luggage we could take as blankets and we made our beds in an empty cage that previously was an exhibit of wolves from the forests of Bavaria. It still smelled of them and their droppings were lying all around like loaves of moldy bread. I barely slept that night because of the noise the rats made. I kept waking on the hour thinking that there was a solitary wolf they had forgotten to remove, hiding in the corner, ready to attack us up at any moment.

'In the morning we were awakened by men's voices and a loud noise like the sound of sawing. It seemed that one of the miniature horses had died and the workers were cutting it into rations. I saw the body of this lovely creature disassembled as if it were a broken toy, its bloody hind quarters leaning up against a wooden fence.

'The same farmer that took us to the town gave us a ride to this city after we both did a day's worth of chores and paid him some money on top of it. I remember that ride through the country, through the farmland that turned from rows of corn into lines of black, wiry grape vines. It was the first time that I was able to see such an amount of land. Green hills that bleached to white. It became my country.

'When we finally arrived here, there was a notice posted in the hospital that proclaimed if one could raise a certain amount of money, a visa could be issued to go to America. My dear friend who was younger than I didn't have enough money so I gave her the rest of mine from my days working as a maid and the next day I said my goodbye to her at the port. I have never seen or heard from her again.

'I found an add for a room for rent at the grocery store and called. The gentleman who was the landlord and recently released from his duty gave me the room, explaining that it would have electricity in a week or so, but despondent as I was, I moved in immediately. I cooked my meals outside using wood and I washed my clothes down the hill in the sea. That room was in the house next door.

Aldo broke in saying, "And in that week, he did provide the electricity. The landlord, you see, is my father."

We broke out in laughter. But he soon became solemn when he explained that his father was quite sick and was staying in the very hospital that was Angèle's passport to freedom. The beginning of her life and the sad chapter that was now unraveling were found at the same location. The hospital was just up the hill overlooking the turquoise Mediterranean.

'We would go to the horse races, even the bullfights when they had them. Or we would just walk along the beach and watch the hills turn orange at day's end. Now they won't even let me bring him meals. And I can only see him for hours a day.

She began to cry. It was now dark outside. The features of the Black Madonna hanging near the window could no longer be made out. We exchanged telephone numbers and addresses. As I prepared for my departure, Angèle offered me a room to stay in but I told her that I had one rented on the other side of town. I promised that the family in America would make contact as soon as possible and that if there was any assistance I could provide.

They both thanked me, Angèle gave me a biscuit for my bus ride back and Aldo hugged me as if I were his long lost son. I didn't want to leave but I had to get back to my small room and the family who was renting it to me. I would be leaving the country in a few days.

Fishbone the cat followed me as far as the front gate and made a sound that sounded like "No" as I closed the lock and waved goodbye.

I caught the bus on the top of the hill near the tall hospital building that stood with most of its lights on. The bus was empty except a couple in the back who held onto each other as if the destination they longed for were sleep. His leather jacket creaked when he moved and she had a delicate silver ring pierced into her nostril. They talked at each stop we came to.

Because you see them everywhere you go. Carrying bread home from the baker's or watching television together in a dimly lit apartment levels above the main street. They travel to foreign countries together or hold jobs in the same office. They talk of vacations they shared in the mountains or times they learned how to ride mopeds along the narrow alleys of the downtown. They share the quotidian intimacies of the day. Their shoes left stepping on each other at the door. Their clothes intertwined in the hamper. A round coffee stain on the pillowcase. Theirs are the secret stories of how they met and fell in love and how they let this love narrate the all too short story of their lives.

When we reached my temporary block of the neighborhood, I signaled for a stop. I was the only one left on the route. I still held the biscuit Angèle gave me in the warm hollow of my pocket. I wondered where the young couple was going. If they lived around here, in an apartment, it couldn't be too far from where I was staying. The doors hissed open and the bus driver turned around. He waved to me and with a wink said, "Until we meet again."

THE NEXT EXIT

"I had wanted to fuck her for forever" were the first words that came into my mind as I looked out on the chocolate mountains behind the billboard of the casino. Years ago, my wife and I had come to this very motel in Winnemucca, Nevada as it was the half way point from Idaho to California. We were moving. In transition. She had a new job. Everything was perfect. The giant sign outside the window blinked a twelve foot version of what I thought we were: "Winners". No neon letters were missing. That's all it said.

W i n n e r s.

That was then and this is then and now. I have returned to Winners Casino in the hellhole that is this place with its one strip featuring a virtual sadness museum of little to no relative history, the cigarette smell of desperation, and oddly, a Portuguese restaurant. I am without wife which is fine because she would be perfect for this place, draped always in black dresses, her favorite non-color. Like the blackness that she enveloped herself in, she is gone. Long gone.

This time I am here to meet the new her. The woman I had been accused of having an affair with. My student. An obsession that never was but an undeniable afterthought, or bugbear . . . what is it when there is something stuck always in the back of the mind? What is that word? A brain splinter? In the desert, words escape me like sweat evaporating.

Her name is Brianna Olsen and indeed she is shorn of Swedish Mormon stock. She has for years written me letters. She took all my classes. She would stand very, very close to me. Cue the Police song. She absolutely would not give up. And since I have nothing now, nothing that is my own, why not? Isn't that what Nevada is for? Beautiful unattainable illusions.

We have agreed to meet here. She is 26 and already divorced. My age is irrelevant but do not think she could be my daughter. More like little sister. Or maybe a niece. A niece I can have my way with and this single factor, not the conversation or what we will eat, terrifies me.

I am drinking watermelon martinis in the bar of the casino. They are very easy to stomach and are a bit weak but there is sugar on the rim. No one of any youth has entered the casino is the last hour. The requisite obese woman with tubes hooked up to her nose and a pseudo-Hawaiian shirt most likely purchased at a flea market. Men whose skin have transformed into beef jerky, slick backed hair, Polo-like shirts, and gold bracelets.

The air is a combination of cigarette smoke, burnt eggs, some kind of melted cheese, and desire. Really, it is kind of delicious. If seedy had a summer address, it would be this. It is absolutely perfect and about eighty seven degrees at night.

She chose to do it this way. In a sense, her life is over in the small Idaho town in which she is condemned to live. She is too beautiful for it. She is an anomaly there and this was obvious when she walked into my classroom wearing fashionable clothes, with her hair done up, and her perfectly manicured toes.

Students from Southeast Idaho Mormon/ranching country normally do not attend classes dressed as models. They don't reek of smoldering sexual desire and smell like a mixture of honeysuckle and vanilla. Her kind of stuff only happens in perverted old man fantasies or seriously dated MTV videos. She was a kind of pornography I could have never predicted.

Cling cling. Ting ting. Wazza wazza wazza. Bweeeep boooo. That is how the stupid take-your-money gambling machines talk. Blinking lights blinking lights blinking lights. Desperation has such a weird demeanor. And I should know.

This was all her idea, for the record. To meet up like this. Sure, I picked the destination as it was a random stop in the life of my wife and me. I should say the lives as it was my illusion that I was sharing one with the person I had been devoted to for over twenty years. There are a few things in this general experience we all share, this mortal coil, and one thing is sure: never be fooled that anything is a mutually exclusive phenomenon. People, no matter how in love, do not share a life. They are always their own solitary creatures.

The weak retreat back into the caves of their own existence and do not desire company. Like a sick dog, they aim to die alone behind a bush or a tree to not be a burden on others. This is the ultimate sadness of being. The audience at the one armed bandits: proof.

It is only in the minds of the crazy ones, the Romantics, who will forever deny this reality. The accursed co-dependent types who want to be with another for every breathing minute, who live in fear of the other's not breathing, who value their existence at such a little price tag that it is negative value if the other is not around– those are the ones who eventually will die of a fabled broken heart. That's my type. I am a seriously fucked up individual. I am what they call the eternal lover.

This is why I have driven six hours and thirty-three minutes. All the way from the East Bay, listening to a.m. radio. Smoking and eating candy bars and drinking horrible gas station coffee. To see what I could not see then. And that would be Brianna's soul.

None of this makes sense. I think that it is so wrong. The premise is fucked up. It's like when, and this is a terrible comparison, when a person, well, mostly a guy but some girls too, look at porn. It's not like they, him, she, we are focused on the naughty bits. We are looking at the photo to see what is in the room, what is on the wall, do we have the same Ikea knick knacks? That kind of thing.

The excitement or dirtiness created by nudity and some melodramatic erotic pose. That's what makes the stuff in the background so interesting. Wondering what the pornographers' subject just had for lunch. Wondering if she has ever truly been in love. Wondering why she holds her hands that way.

My phone just lit up. She texted me. She will be here soon. In an hour or so. She had a bad drive. The freeway was windy. There is still snow on the mountains coming her way. Said she passed a whore house named Donna's Ranch in the middle of nowhere. Said she's never seen one before.

~

I can feel the day's heat creeping into the entrance of the casino. The entrance is carpeted in bowling alley style motifs and the lobby branches into a restaurant, the front desk, and the small black hole of the gaming room.

I tried my luck at a slot machine. Spin, spin spin. A banana, cherries, a bust. An omen. Or just dumb luck.

She is in the back of my head always. Not just a sexual obsession. It's the fact that no one can save her. There is nothing better than rescue. Even if you cannot save yourself. She is always in the back of my head. She is literally there now.

Hands touch my shoulders. Hands heavily manicured and as light as undone bras. She is here. We are here.

It's the beginning of a B movie and a 1970s porno with subtitles. The subtitles say in 12 different languages "mistake". The subtitles, like the awkwardly funky music, play in both of our heads at the same time, slightly out of synch.

Green as the smell of sagebrush in a rainstorm she has grown in total isolation. She has no idea what to do with her body.

She touches my neck. I can feel manicured and maybe even fake fingernails. I turn around and look up but before I do she has kissed me hard and snug on the cheek, the way a semi-familiar auntie would and she smells of hair product and strawberry lip gloss.

"I can't believe it", she says.

"I can't believe you're here."

Idolization of Sacajawea. Long black hair dyed into oblivion. Some kind of glittery halter top, pinkish but I cannot tell in these lights. Really tight painted on black jeans or are they some fabric I don't understand? A white frilly overshirt that is see through. The edges of a black bra. Open toe leather sandal platforms.

Be kind the gods of irony and let me die now. There could never be a moment better than this. The long desert drive. Years of thinking about her. Slightly buzzed on three gin and tonics I didn't even need to mention. The somewhat vague yet recognizable late eighties music in the background.

Seeing her live standing here, touchable. Her wanting to touch me. Wanting.

"I think I've been in love with you for so long" is what we are both thinking although we must both be so very wrong.

~

Blackout of the drearily mundane. Time has passed. I now sit in the Alameda County Courthouse in the east bay of San Francisco waiting for a divorce proceeding. It wasn't that night that put this into motion. Nothing ever happened. At least nothing truly worth remembering or regretting.

We went back to the room with its swamp boat fan of an air conditioner blowing the place more windy than frigid. I couldn't get over the pattern of the room's carpeting: blue, red, green tartan. There were as expected, indeterminate stains. Not blood, not coffee, not motor oil but something in the category of ugly permanence.

She told me of her problems. Of how she would cut herself just to feel something, anything. About the boys she loved and fucked to, in her own words, "no avail". It's never good to love or fuck to no avail.

She cried and talked about the tattoos she wanted. About the boys who treated her like shit. I stared at her hair. It was her whole persona. I looked at her young, sloping boobs. Directly. Without shame.

She grabbed my arm. She tried to kiss me.

I started to let her. And then I just couldn't. I ordered a pizza and a salad and the salad was put on a pizza crust because it was Nevada and that stood for gourmet. We laughed.

I held her as she told me more stories of her terrible life, which were all off premise and born from errors of perception, how young people think and cannot see in depth or beyond their sleek sexy bodies, and she fell asleep in my arm. How she even quietly snored.

The next morning we said goodbye over a disgustingly greasy egg and waffle breakfast and she was gone from my life forever.

Divorce, contrary to customary belief, is a game that children play. Adults re-enacting child's play.

You do not know me and I do not know you; let's get that straight. Just like the beauty queen I chose to meet left of the center of the middle of nowhere, in the golden west of utter desolation, the wife, like all people in fact, men and women, friend and foe, cannot not fathom a person like me.

My attraction to the emptiness of sage brush country, to unnamed mountain peaks no one ever desires to hike, to roadside greasy spoons with their depressingly limited menus with only a promise of a malted milkshake and the consequences of knife-sharp heartburn, to the endless highways littered with the refuse of afterthought, was all just my addiction to plain desire. The desire to be forever in transition. Never giving a fuck if the center cannot hold.

So the three-ring circus of divorce is what I get for being who I am or who I refuse to ever be.

This has to be why of the few things I have ever owned that the person who now publicly hates me has kept my mini version, a novelty lamp, of the Las Vegas sign, complete with blinking lights. Though I am gone, my aesthetic remains.

I have traveled from here to here. The secret is that there is no there there or anywhere. It only makes sense that I have located paradise in a semi-arid landscape tamed by out of control expansion and the white buildings that try to hide the dirt that is money are covered, if you look closely, with grime.

Crime and punishment the old man wrote and if you ever end up anywhere near the bay of San Francisco, a body of water that mocks the desert that surrounds, you know you have been convicted and have been sentenced to a most picturesque Alcatraz.

That's what makes it so bad: it's all so pretty from a distance but you cannot ever have it. You can only look but never touch. And never know.

That after twenty-three years, she sits down in the hall, nervous, wearing black because of course it's slimming, out of love once again, is only appropriate. She should be scared. Divorce is the new marriage.

Yes, I could have loved the beauty queen. Hell, I could even live in a place like Reno. That is because I am condemned to be a person who is all about the other. The strange thing is is that mostly anyone will do. I am that addicted to loving.

It is the desolated places that I long for. The motel rooms without a view. The towns in which one can only wonder what people do there to make a living, intersected by a silent railroad track. Let's call it Bridgeport, CA in this instance. These places are everywhere. Full of people who have given up on wondering why they are there.

My glory will come within the hour. I have my memories of her and her and her. I have a vague notion of the next one. It is all I need.

Like an aging rock star I await that magical moment when I get to say the one thing I am famous for. My swan song. My state's motto. The words that fall off my tongue like prayer. I guess they are "I don't".

As I walk into the court room Breanna texts me:

:(. . .

interlude

THE BOOK OF BROKEN DREAMS

The day, an ordinary one. An ordinary day in a string of ordinary days. Morning made it so. Ingredients of a recipe endlessly followed: touch of sun, fog stuck in the crevasses of lolloping fields, cloud bank growing plumes in the distance. Clip-clop clip-clop clip-clop of horses pulling carts. Hay and supplies. A gas truck pulling into the station from wherever gas came. Nobody much thought about these things. They just sort of happened. They just sort of happened everyday.

The town was still waking up. Only the bakery's lights were burning. Steam from hot bread rained down its windows. Pamela Grady, the baker, worked through the night, her arms covered up to her elbows with powder and dough. Her daughter Emily helped her finish the nearly perfect pastries they created. They had to have just the proper amount of icing. The pattern of frosting was what caught the customer's eye, Pamela would say, twirling her index finger in the air. Her daughter looked, thought a bit, and attempted to add the right amount of filling or decoration to the cakes, like her mother showed, but rarely to any avail. They ended eating the ones she botched. Pamela's once tiny frame was now surrounded by one hundred and eighty-nine pounds. And steadily climbing.

The quiet of the night slowly seeped out of the crossroads of the four block downtown and into the cattle lots and miles of planted gardens and farm fields that sidled the country. Soon the children would appear from the porches of their Victorian houses and make their way towards school, talking loudly and making noises at the horses. Human horse noises. Soon, tourists would begin to arrive to search for treasures that a town of this antiquity still sequestered, and from time to time, sold.

A town that had only the past to keep it alive. There were six antique stores that sold everything from strangely shaped farm implements to grand pianos, to signposts of the old railroad lines, to landscapes embroidered into rugs. Of course there was the usual requirements of any grouped existence: a drug store, a sundry, two restaurants that served two different kinds of the same food, a grocery, a dentist, a hardware, a doctor's, a veterinarian, and nine different churches. Mass, at any of them, was never ever crowded.

It was the definition of sleep come awake and turned into a place to live. There weren't any major interstates within a thirty mile vicinity. Not much in the way of novelty passed through. Hills and dales and a few streams bordered by poplars and some oak, but mostly unnamed weed trees, willows, maples, poplars. This valley looked like the next valley and the previous one, if a traveler even would venture to lift his eyes from the winding road that led from wherever he came to the nowhere he had to cross to reach a destination like the Mississippi or a metropolis that didn't want to be one. Omaha of no one's wishing.

Even brightly colored pamphlets about the cosmos and the "origination" of sin went unread. They cluttered the laundromat, left by local Jesus freaks. The townspeople had all heard it before and were waiting for a different kind of savior. Or a new distillation of grace. Or that one fat lottery ticket.

What made this parcel of cleared-out trees any different from the orchards and streams of poplars growing in ribbons among squares of purposeful cropland was the idea of commerce, or at least, of growth. The promise of money built a cross of pavement that served as the town's one and only intersection. Buildings that decorated it like ancient ornaments on a Christmas tree were frozen in a frontier style of practicality. It were as if an old tintype of a mining town had somehow survived among the groves of fir and bur oak. Perhaps an expedition encountered hostile Indians who decimated the male contingent and became assimilated by the German women's beauty. The new people that formed from this mixture celebrated their fateful meeting by staying at the place of their initial rendezvous and blood mingling. But who knows?

Buildings were resolutely made of stone and a few were untouched—left to stand in the buff of their natural color: a limestone yellow-white. Most were painted once a decade. The general store was barn red. The bank was an unsullied white. The hardware store was painted brown so it looked like wood. The bakery, grey and green; the butcher's was glossy black, probably to mask the stain of blood. The few shops that sold distinctive knick knacks combined brick and painted window frames in their ornate, turn of the century edifices. A passerby wouldn't notice anything exceptional about this town and it habitants were responsible for its upkeep of anonymity. They liked it that way. Information one doesn't know is useless anyway.

There were other buildings here and there off the main X. Near the park there was the veterinarian's: a new single-level building that had a wall of pure window so sick animals could look out and see birds landing in the park's grass across the street. Cats sat so close that they made little circles of steam in front of their whiskered faces.

There were many antique stores housed in buildings of neighborhood homes, which were antiques themselves. These places never really made a profit but they kept a few of the town's older couples busy sorting out relics of a better past. Blankets made from the clothes of early settlers, horseshoes garnered from the passing by pony express, a finger of a Mexican general kept in an old tobacco tin, beads used as currency by the native tribes, religious objects looking like implements made for the destruction of pigs, the head of a jackelope on a board with marbles for eyes, tapestries of Jesus enacting various scenes of the apocrypha, tools made long ago for such reasons as lemon squeezing and pillow case folding and removing burrs from horses' tails. A wealth of objects no longer used.

This town, located to the west of somewhere, was a storage bin for unremembered memories waiting to be found or undiscovered. You could say that, but really, this place was a sleepy amalgamation of post-pioneer architecture and a living display of the run down. True, a few families that believed enough in the name of the town (rumored to be that of a solitary roaming buffalo untamable by man) to promulgate its existence with a new crop of blonde-haired babies every so many years did just that with goodness and kindness to make the stretch of fields and woods comfortably habitable throughout its five pronounced seasons. Always an Indian summer. And that was the one aspect that enlivened the otherwise silent, dreamy streets: the laughter of children.

At given times of the day, usually in conjunction with the morning and afternoon breaks from school, children whisked through the alleys and sidewalks and matted down trails through the fields in a blur of agitated energy. Red windbreaker jackets and blue baseball caps. Yellow and white ribbons tied into ponytails. Few of these children would stay in the town once given the opportunity to break free from the innocence of youth. The big cities, pulsating with neon and false light, were a day's and a night's drive away. They usually took years from which to return.

The only other corner of interest in the town itself was its sole art gallery. Perhaps five percent of the residents knew of its existence, on a good day. It was tucked away on the end of Q street and the gravel road that led to Arthur Vinton's experimental cornfield. He called it that because every season he tried a different brand of seed and watered the rows with different amounts of water while keeping notebooks detailing his revolutionary growing methods. He would come into town at the end of the growing season and sell his husks of maize door to door, explaining to prospective buyers how each kernel held within it the sweet taste of sunlight. He was fifty-eight years old and had been married five times.

His third wife, tired of living in stacks of notebooks and files papers and daily accounts of the weather's effect on his stalks that Arthur wound together with old shoelaces and sometimes hastily crafted into furniture, began throwing them out the bedroom window into a pile of burning deadwood.

For about a week, Arthur didn't miss his records. He exploded into a fury when he saw pages of documentation in his own handwriting being blown about his fields, hopelessly charred, barely readable. He divorced her one month prior to harvest and let her leave with their one child, a station wagon, and all of the real furniture. Before leaving town, she stopped by the art gallery to say goodbye to her friends. Her name was Lindy.

About the only people who ever ventured into the gallery, which was called simply The Art Gallery, were friends. It was a big building, a former welding shop, that contained various rooms of artistic meddling. A boiler room to run a metal-melting oven, a well-lit studio for painting, the various machinery needed for bronze casting- a home-made slag oven, wood and metal working tools, old welding equipment that functioned when the humidity wasn't too high, an actual gallery, and office, and a wax melting/all purpose lunch room.

What the artists who worked there had constructed was a cooperative to work on commissioned works of art, when they got them, and then their own endeavors. What they fabricated was more unneeded stuff. Beautiful unneeded stuff. Mostly sculptures, sometimes portraits, what people considered "strange paper weights", even occasionally state-commissioned statues in bronze and signs and plaques in iron. The business never made a cent in the black, but the artists survived. And the town let them be.

None of the artists lived in the town proper. They would commute from their low-rent apartments in the smaller and larger surrounding villages. This contributed to the lasting presence of the Gallery. The dirties, as the townspeople called them, with their eccentric lifestyles evident in the empty cans of beer and bottles of cheap wine by the morning garbage can, would have been shunned if they chose to inhabit the second floor apartments of the downtown. Sixty hours a week the lights were lit. Pounding sounds, loud music, laughter, and arguments could be heard inside. Routinely, the boiler would blow, or there would be a small explosion, the type that occurs when molten bronze is poured into a wet mold, and the noise would echo through the streets and ruffle the thick leaves of the oak trees. The attention paid to such an outburst would usually be a three line paragraph in the local paper. *The Gallery blew its top again today. No one was hurt and the melee was caused by a malfunctioning air compressor. Rex said it was nothing that couldn't be fixed with some tape and a clothes hanger.*

Once a week an Amish farmer would dare to visit the Gallery, inquire to what was going on inside, and linger around the nude sculptures on display. He would rub his beard while offering words of advice about how the co-op should produce something in demand like horseshoe nails, try to sell some of his brown eggs, then leave with a crooked smile. For the Amish, it was speculated by the artists, the Gallery's corner of strangeness was just bizarre enough and functional to not raise any questions of appropriateness. Every so often, radical elders would threaten to cut the power lines of the town because it was too near the verge of modernization, as evidence of its corruptness: the business of icon-making. But they pretty much left the Gallery alone. It was rumored that Amish spies had come into town under the cover of night to peer into the windows of the shop, just to stay updated and make sure that no idolatry was being manufactured. One assumes that they didn't quite recognize the idealized nudity of the figures in bronze as the same as of their wives and daughters, that is, if they ever looked at the naked whiteness of a woman's body in the light of the day.

There were seven artists who worked consistently and feverishly at the Gallery. This is not counting the twenty or so artisans who visited the premises for consultation, assistance, sometimes to borrow the tools of production, and or to visit. The hilly countryside cradled many independent spirits who took their hobbies of making custom made garlic presses and bolo ties and lawn ornaments or parts for outdated tractors as an Art. Often the Gallery could pinch some money out of these eccentrics and could even learn a new technique, or at least get some information. Like where scrap metal could be found for cheap.

The Gallery didn't need much to function. Some clients. Raw materials of glue, chemicals for rubber mold making, wax, welding rods, electricity, gas, iron, shipments of bronze when the accounts could be made to look in the plus. Sunlight, long hours, the tools that had naturally accumulated there, and an interest in doing one's own thing, a taste for independence. The Gallery was in the business of making art– the dreams of other people who couldn't dream, or just didn't, or forgot how. The crucial element to it's existence in a certain place in a certain time was the artists themselves, who through hours of sweating in dust and metal filings, plaster powder, cleaning oily paint brushes and breathing the fumes of paint thinner, managed to create and make into things, their thoughts, ideas, come true.

The Dream of Alexandria

Alex, as everyone called her, had a painter's face. She could, in a look, create a tableau of a facial expression that summed up her feelings at any given moment. Mostly it was one of doubtful contentedness. Having recently been hired as a general work-about, she was the newest mystery to happen upon the Gallery.

She struggled as a starving artist, living in the university town twenty-five miles north. From time to time, she would display her paintings in the small galleries reserved for the work of students and she, from time to time, would enroll in a class, usually one that had nothing to do with painting—the history of book-making, or a class in nature writing.

She drove a broken down Chevy Impala, colored the ugliest shade of green-brown that there ever was, so terrible that people would ask her if it was a coat of primer and when she would be re-painting it, soon?, and what color. The trunk was tied closed with knitting yarn. It contained frames and rolled up canvasses. The interior was littered with soda pop cans, one of the main staples of Alex's diet: half-crushed and flung among old sweaters, shirts, other remnants stained with oil colors. The heat didn't work nor did the air conditioning, there was only an a.m. radio that sometimes functioned and the car both leaked and burned oil. It cost her about thirty bucks a week to keep it running, gas and motor oil, a fan belt ruptured every two months and sometimes, when she couldn't afford to buy a new one, she would use a sleeve of one of the many shirts she drove around with to do the job. It would usually last until the next paycheck.

She was an independent spirit, but like everyone else, not as free as she wanted to be. That was one of her main complaints, having to work at the Gallery part-time because her other part time work for the city– stabilizing old wooden telephone poles—had good benefits, but she couldn't make ends meet. Painting supplies are expensive and that is why she drank liquid sugar for breakfast/lunch with perhaps a yogurt and ate simply one meal a day. It was a diet of necessity, one she had no choice but become used to. It kept her going.

The others at the Gallery would bring in food for her and she always accepted. She ate real slow, enjoying every bite and saying how good food tastes especially when other people make it. Especially when other people made it just for her.

As a co-worker, she was an invaluable intermediary. She mixed rubber concoction for molds, shipped out works of art, ordered supplies, talked to visitors, and her specialty was applying patinas to the pieces of bronze that had been sold, finished, and lined up on a wood table ready for their metallic hints of coloring. Green, blue, and charred brown were her favorite mixtures and no one did it better or more delicately.

She would stand at the table in the work area of the building, don yellow plastic gloves, adjust her glasses right, and hold a few paint-brushes in her mouth and not speak to anyone, or look up, till the jobs were done. It was the closet thing to getting paid to do her chosen trade, and she knew that these moments were bliss. So did everyone else and she was left unbothered.

It was speculated that Alex thought in color. She wore a differ-ent shirt to work each day, one that reflected how she felt. When she wore her black t-shirt, it would be a day of intense concentration and no joking. The best days were when she wore her long sleeve white smock, stained with all sorts of paints and chemicals. Those days she would talk of her paintings on the easel as she would say, what her plans for the weekend were, friends she once knew, and bits and pieces of her childhood in the medium-sized river town a hundred and fifty miles away. Those days she would even talk about her two trips to New Orleans, her city of reverie and nostalgia, a place where she wanted to live to begin a series of paintings of the beautiful, run down doors of that city. And how she could live in a house modeled from the crypts they had in the cemeteries down there. She liked old things. Even Nora's near-the-verge-of-death Great Dane, who was at last count, turning sixteen.

Alex had three paintings hanging in the gallery. Recent ones that she could afford to have framed and make ready to be sold. One was of her backyard and featured, if one ventured to look close enough at it, her cat stalking birds among other blatantly normal backyard things. Tomato plants growing in conical trestles of wire. A lawnmower covered in wet, cut grass. One tree. A chewed-up dog frisbee. Lots of grass and wild flowering weeds. Rocks that snakes loved to hide under. A patio with a picnic bench. It was titled "Summer" and sold for two hundred dollars.

The other painting was of a young boy or girl, it was hard to tell and made little difference, catching lightning bugs in a jar. Or trying to. There weren't any bugs in the topless jar and merely the movement of a figure reaching upward and the few lights flittering away, into the upper right hand corner of the canvass, of the bugs that could have also been stars. The style of the painting was what can be gestured at as muffled, the figure was fuzzy, the background a thick dark color of night, no attempt at true perspective or realism in the sense of things and how light actually played upon them, except starlight. This one was everyone's favorite, probably Alex's too, but she never admitted it. She said her favorite picture was the next one she would make, the ideal painting stuck somewhere in the crook of her mind and visible only to its eye.

When asked about this certain work, she could be tricked into telling the story she might sometimes tell, about the first time she was lead to making her visions real, back when she was a little girl growing up on a farm.

First warm days of Spring when granma came to visit and everyone in the family had a cold. Worse kind of colds come when the weather's turning towards hot. Always the hard labor of repairing falling apart buildings, milking the cows, cleaning moss from the pond, patching up a weather torn roof— none of it could get done because everyone was feeling so low. Granma decided that what the household needed was a huge batch of a chicken soup, made and kept and frozen in plastic bags so the remedy could be taken any-time in the year. Without telling anyone what her plan was, she went out to the coop and started whacking off the heads of any fowls she could get her bony hands around. When I got up that morning, 'round sevenish, out my second floor bedroom window— unholy noises and the not yet corpses of five or so headless birds running around the yard. One even got airborne and crashed in my window leaving a handprint of blood. Granma came out of the coop, covered in a spray of red, and carrying a butcher's knife. With her other gnarled, sun-browned hand, she waved at me. My blood covered granma smiling and waving at me. She wanted me to come down and start plucking feathers from the still-warm bodies. She was smiling, waving at me, droplets of fat and blood in her grey hair.

The scene, the vignette of slaughter, as she calls it, still bore a meaning she couldn't quite get at. It was the subject of the third painting titled "Red Afternoon". Alex would seldom speak of what she did in her free time, other than paint, and the other artists never pressed her on this point. They themselves rarely got together outside of the Gallery because everyday was a sort of party. They could drink beer, smoke, indulge in pots of cheap coffee, talk for hours if the work they were doing if the work that day allowed them to form into a group. When they did go out, it was to the pub down the street, the only real bar in town that served beer, liquor, greasy fried food, and had a single pool table and even a television set that people looked at but never watched.

The Gallery would hold a weekly planning meeting at the pub. Alex would order a soda, out of politeness, and watch the guys light up their cigarettes. She quit smoking the day her best friend did, about a year back. The weekly meetings always quickly soured into gripe sessions, vague plans for current projects, and an escape from the grime of the Gallery, and proved to be for Alex a devilish temptation. As much as she had to paint to stay sane and alive, she wanted to smoke.

One miserably cold morning in the opening months of December, Alex didn't show up for work. It was one of those days when the radio announcers can't help but use the word "bitter" to describe the chill. Her car broke down on the two-lane highway that led from the college town north of the lonely farm ville. This highway paralleled the bigger interstate heading south but it was about forty or more miles away from its larger sibling. The road was infamous for traffic of farm tractors and slow moving trucks that opted for its less crowded going. It also skirted through the mesmerizing hills and dales between one river valley and the next and was regarded as the prettier route for driving. The problem though with beauty is that not many people really care too much for it in the modern world. Not many cars were filling up the lanes that morning, especially at nine thirty a.m. when Alex's Chevy began to sputter, shake and cough, with three idiot lights illuminating the dash board at once. She coasted it over to the shoulder, tried starting it again to no avail, turned the radio off realizing that it wasn't a bad battery, and almost began to cry.

It was twenty-two below with the wind chill, she remembered the disembodied voice say only a few minutes ago. She had a scarf and some yarn mittens, that were more so socks, with her. The walk into town would be twelve or so miles. Fortunately, the sun was out but the ground was covered with a light snowfall that had completely frozen over, without melting a bit, so it looked like the fields were covered in white sand dunes. When she got out of the car, the snow gave way under her footfalls with the sound of breaking glass. Nobody passed by. She was surrounded by miles of ditches, empty fields, and about a mile away tucked into a hollow of woods and a frozen crick, a small badly-built shack. She decided to head in that direction to ask for help.

She hopped over a wire fence and trekked through a field, some-times sinking up to her knees in ditches of hard snow. Powdery under-neath its hard skin, the snow began to trickle into her socks and melt with a sting. She was only wearing tennis shoes. She tried aiming for the hoof prints of horses to avoid wading in the stuff; where the horses were now, it couldn't be seen. The wind was scorching her face red and freezing solid the liquid in her eyes and nose, but she pressed on with thoughts of frostbite and that Jack London story about building a fire. She could always go back and wait in the car, put on the hazards, and sleep until somebody stopped, she thought. But first she would try to find someone since no one could possibly know of her whereabouts.

When she got to the house, she noticed that the snow had not been scraped from the front porch. She knocked on the storm door. It was covered in plastic, like the windows. It looked like whoever covered the windows ran out of material and had to resort to covering one of them with saran wrap and duct tape. In the window she peered and saw a blurry vision of the inside. Wooden floors, a couch, a table with a chair, and a bed covered by a quilt. It looked like the interior was being kept as a museum piece, a room of a living history farm or some such curiosity, it was perfect in arrangement and cleanliness even though the outside was rickety and thrown together with old boards, strips of aluminum siding.

She knocked and knocked on the door calling out *hello, is there anyone in there?*

No reply. She thought about breaking in to use the telephone but couldn't tell if the thick black lines leading into an upper corner of the roof were simply electrical. She gave up and headed back to the empty car. A flock of geese arrowed over head, calling wildly, and she wondered why they were heading south so late. And where, exactly, were they going?

Half way back to the desolate highway, two cars drove by. She motioned with her raw hands for them to stop. The drivers were crouched down low, driving fast to speed out of the cold and warm their engines quickly. The road didn't encourage travelers to idly look about the countryside, especially in winter, when getting from one heated enclosure to the next is a priority. They passed her with fast diminishing sounds of departure.

She almost couldn't open the frozen shut car door, had to kick the handle twice, almost slipping on the ice underneath. The heat of the engine melted the sludge underneath the car, and in the meantime, it had re-frozen. She got back in, turned the blower on to be comforted, at least, by sound of air moving, and put the radio on a news station. She dreamt she heard the report of her death. One young woman found in an abandoned car along highway one, hands frozen stiff to the steering wheel.

Alex thought what an interesting subject for a series of paintings. Victims of the cold. A series of portraits of people frozen to death in the surroundings of their last predicament. A woman darning socks by a broken radiator. A farmhand fallen in a field, covered in buckets of solidified milk. Two teenagers, naked and dead lying on top of one another in a snowdrift, a blanket frozen hard under and over them. Herself in her faithful car, hard as the frozen rags and shirts she was now using as blankets. She thought about the effect of cold on paints, if she should try to dry freeze some of her works, a solemn landscape of a lake covered in ice, then chilled with nitrogen to heighten the paint's texture. She thought of the color of her blood at the moment, how red the circulating red was, how blue the oxygen hungry blue pigment was running through her cold limbs, escaping the outer lands of her fingers and toes to rejoin the warmth of her heart. The tears welling up in her eyes weren't cold.

She thought that someday she would be in another place, that one day she might have a job doing what she wanted to do, being a museum guide, or the owner of a real gallery that exhibited her own paintings. That she would live in a warm place like the swamps of Louisiana where she'd have a cabin in the bayou with a wood-burning stove that never, for an instant, would be without a fire. How she missed her friends at the Gallery, who were probably missing her right at this moment, how in one studio a crock pot would be melting dark brown wax for proto-sculptures, making the area warm with the smell of burning tires. Splashes of it like chocolate on the walls and floor. How if she had a cigarette she would smoke it to taste fire, ash, smoke, the heat of tobacco in her shrinking lungs. How evil snow was because it is white, without color. How her skin was whitening in the cold air, losing color. Before passing out, her last thought was this: *Aquamarine.*

The Dream of Sam and Louise

Sam was like the wind. There's no better way of explaining it. He was an all-around artist. A painter, a sculptor, a caricaturist, a cartoonist, and mostly a line drawer. His best, most intense work, were pictures of country life, in ink and pencil. One has to start out simply when trying to capture Sam, or a picture of him, in a moment of stasis. He never did portraits.

He was part everything. Irish, German, Amish, American Indian, Mexican, and only he knows what else. It was something he bragged about. He looked like a mutt, what he referred to himself as most of the time: long black, graying hair tied in a pony tail, a big wild nose like a horse's, black eyes, a mustache, glasses; he always wore an army jacket. He chain-smoked generic cigarettes and the room would fill with their scent before a person could turn around and see him standing in a corner, leaning on the wall, looking you straight in the eye.

He part-timed at the Gallery to earn some extra cash and made his living mostly on arts and crafts shows around the midwest and the west, occasionally the upper tier of the south. He was the definition of a loner. Nobody at the Gallery really knew him well; some thought others knew him better, and those others thought the other others knew him even better. They were all wrong. This was how Sam wanted it. He existed in the margins of what other people thought. Half man, half spirit.

Another way a person could tell that Sam had arrived was by sound. If he decided to come in early, about six a.m., the building would fill with the sound of either Hank Williams, the original, or the Beatles. These were Sam's two tapes that he kept with him in his army jacket pocket. The theme songs, or background music, of his life that everyone, by his sporadic presence, learned to recognize and expect when he appeared.

Lately, though, Sam wasn't showing up much. And when he did, he behaved more mysterious than usual. It was rumored that he was carrying a gun somewhere in the green folds of his army jacket. The logic went something like this: his current girlfriend, Louise, was involved with a man in Omaha. This no-name man was running with a pack of partyers come Satan worshipers. One night, when they were roaming the streets of a sleepy midwestern metropolis, they needed some cash and happened to find a wadful in the cash register of a gas station. The clerk of the station didn't want to disperse of the money, and ended up with a tire-iron buried about an inch and a half in his head. Louise was a witness to the crime, even though she was drunk and out of her proper senses. She was told that they chloroformed the man and she pretended to believe it.

The band of devil worshippers didn't give her a cut of the take and she began to hint around that she knew something about the latest unsolved story in the newspapers. Not much happened in the city; to know about a headline as strange as "Gas Station Man Found with Broken Skull" gave her a rush of power. She began dropping hints at the beauty salon and the coffee house.

She worked in a bead and home-made jewelry shop from which, when the day was over, she would leave to meet the locals at a biker pub called Nightshift. When her few girl friends began to shy away from her, she knew she was saying too much, too soon. Her boyfriend had left a message on her machine to meet him by the river, another favorite drinking rendezvous, that night. Instead, she went home with Sam, who was blowing through town and had stopped to get a brew and shoot some pool. Of course, she told him everything right before they stopped on the shoulder of the interstate to consummate their relationship in the spacious back of his van. Immediately afterwards, in the breath of quickly smoked cigarettes, he decided that it would be safest if she were to run away with him until things cooled down. Sam and his ideas.

So she did. Sam found her a part-time job at a local jewelry repair shop and silversmith's. The business, inside the owner's garage, was on the other side of town, near the highway, so she could watch which cars came in, drove through, and left. She began crafting watch bands out of metal, earrings, and pendants that borrowed motifs from her one time colleagues: five pointed stars, ram horns, pitchforks, numerological series inscribed into arm and wristbands. She took to wearing big hats and long flowing dresses. The townspeople hardly noticed her, even though she was supplying their children with ornamentation of Satanic cults, cleverly incorporated into what they regarded as harmless trinkets. The folks at the Gallery called her Glenda the good witch when she came in, ever so rarely and usually with Sam, to visit.

The two of them would hang around the gallery, hinting at their latest exploits like how they combined their booths at an art fair— Sam selling his pictures, as he called them, and Louise selling her hand-crafted jewelry, usually to the girlfriends of the men who were interested in buying a drawing to fill up that creative hole in their own manhood. Interesting how people filtered into their booth that contained not only art but the artist too, an intimate setting with hardly any natural barriers. It was so easy for people to walk by the Gallery, check out the decor of bronze pouring pots filled with geraniums, cars lined in a row, and cigarette butts crushed haphazardly and swept into the cracks of the sidewalks, then peek into the dusty windows to see bronzes placed all about the room, paintings hanging crooked on the walls, and then dismiss the place as workshop for busy elves. But at a craft show, it was all there in the open: the work, the crummy display materials of painted plywood and peg board, the artist slumped behind it looking as at ease as a dinner rabbit.

Men, with their women, would file by, eyes on the works, the woman's eyes on the artist. Sometimes they'd stop, retrace their steps, go back and drum up a conversation. Sometimes they'd find a little landscape that would be just perfect for a hall, or work office, and they would try to haggle a better price. Sometimes Sam would play along when he was real thirsty and needed beer money. Usually though he'd turn his head and say Come back when you're serious. He had a way about him of making people feel inferior to not necessarily him, but his art, and this phenomenon helped him to sell his pictures.

His pictures: Indians crossing the hills of their native lands; a lightning rod attached to a barn, landscapes with defunct, eroding buildings; views of hidden corners of the woods; a pictorial inventory of the tools of the Amish; down to earth compositions rooted in reality.

It was rumored, mostly by Louise, that he'd begun a portrait series of her which included nude charcoal sketches that he would never sell but most likely display at the Gallery. The guys couldn't wait for this because Louise, underneath her layers of Indian textiles and streams of fabric she bought at festivals, sported a figure worth concealing. Her skin was freckled white, her hair red, and her body thin and nymph-like. Sam was mesmerized by her very footfall, this was obvious to all. About the only times he dropped by the Gallery when alone was when he needed the phone to call Louise. And he used the phone in the back room, and even then, spoke real low.

When Louise visited, sometimes without Sam, she never revealed much about herself. Even when a local newspaper did an article about her, against Sam's better judgment, it didn't say much about who she was and dwelled mostly on what she did: jewelry. She made such beautiful things of pure simplicity: silver earrings based on Aztec designs, arm bands and bracelets, and anklets of gold metal, watch bands of silver incorporating only a hint of turquoise, rings of metal in the shapes of thread. She was a magician of things, trinkets and amulets that could put the eyes under a momentary spell.

They were in love with the thought of each other. Sam gave her the space and seclusion she needed, and she took care of him. The morning Sam awoke to find a dagger spray-painted on the door of his house, that wasn't at first visible from the road due to the oak trees, he knew it was over. Or, it had just begun. The pack of demon lovers not only had found out where Louise had fled, but who was helping her out. And they must have had a connection in this part of the country to have been able to locate his home address. At least, that's what was surmised at the Gallery.

In the bright morning light, Sam first smelled the scent of paint, which was what turned him around, opened his eyes to the crudely drawn knife, the handle filled in black, that ran the length of the door. Along the representation of the blade were the markings: 6 or 7, and an eye symbol. Sam had no idea what it meant, other than trouble.

He came into the Gallery early that day, forsaking his music, smoking twice the amount of cigarettes as usual, and phoning places. He left his van running outside. His gun was in his leg holster, he implied. He said only a few words to Rex, who was already up and at it near seven thirty a.m., tore down the road map of the U.S. that was pasted up with dirty, fingerprinted scotch tape by the phone. The door closed with its stupid jangling bell and a stream of Sam's smoke swirling at its back, too late to disperse into the outside air.

Sometimes the people at the Gallery get a postcard from Sam and Louise. Usually its from a cheap motel, privately owned, off a major interstate. Most recently, they've been arriving from Montana, Wyoming, Idaho, and Washington. They never say much other than *We're all right and thinking of you* or *the food here is terrible.* Sometimes the backs of the postcards are filled up with a little sketch of the surrounding arid lands that Sam does when Louise is driving. Some times they have splotches of dried wine, car grease, ashes, and once even, a smudge of lipstick.

It's been four months since they've left and nobody knows exactly where they went. Or keep going to. It's guessed that they're selling their works at small-time fairs, or even businesses, in tourist mountain towns, and living off what they earn. A few times back, a man stopped by the Gallery asking for Sam, saying that he was interested in "some art stuff" so it is supposed that they are on the run. Raymond was telling everyone how these satanic cults have members in every city in the United States and they operate a sort of antiquated network of information and contact, so Sam and Louise could never really stay anywhere for too long because these weirdos would always catch up. Raymond himself is pretty paranoid about mostly anything, having confessed to sleeping with a Swiss army knife under his pillow "just in case." He could be right, though. That would explain why there's those photos of missing kids on milk cartons, Nora added. They got to get human sacrifices somehow and kids are easy to capture. Since Louise was a witness to a crime and could identify some of the members, she had to be put out of the equation. Minds were beginning to become creatively burdened by the possibilities of criminal behavior.

What Sam and Louise were doing was this: driving. They were driving to wherever the road would lead them. They'd stop at gas stations off the highway to fill up the tank and buy whatever substitute food the place was selling. Almost always there would be the thick-skulled night clerk, with a mess of never combed hair, talking to a band of local rowdies, the kind of guys that continued the leather jacket tradition and had little confederate flags on the antennas of their seventies gas guzzlers. After picking up the odd bag of chips, or if they were daring, a hot dog or plasticy microwaved slice of something vaguely resembling pizza, Sam would head out of the place with his eyes in the rearview. Devil worshippers and white trash went hand in hand considering outward appearances, he thought.

They were driving because it felt good. Humm of the engine, music crackling on the radio, the window open enough to let a thin band of constant cigarette smoke escape. Louise would put her feet on his lap and he would massage them when she wasn't expecting.

They didn't know if they would ever go back, wherever back was. They could pick up and move off to anywhere they wanted. They didn't need much, only each other. They didn't expect to see anyone they knew ever again because, as dreamers must do in the waking hours, Sam and Louise were living their dream.

The Dream of Raymond

He was your basic paranoid type. A painter. In this vein, a realist. Portraits of locals was his thing. And objects. His one really good effort was a study of a bed sheet. A white bed sheet. It looked like it was actually tossed within the frame. People would go up and touch it, much to his consternation.

He did landscapes too. Always something tranquil. A farmhouse, a stream, a plot of green land. He wasn't painting regularly since he hooked up with the Gallery because Rex worked him to death. Rex antagonized him like living hell for reasons no one knows. Probably it was because Raymond was so damn tall, nearly seven feet, and Rex was only five foot eight. Reason enough.

Raymond didn't have much quotidian luck. He hated getting up in the morning, came into work late, stayed until seven or eight at night, ate, slept, visited the bathroom for lengthy intervals of time at the Gallery, sort of made his job into his second home. Indeed the Gallery was a cooperative, a funny title that is destined to never work in such a manner, but Rex and Nora were living in the back of the place, so it was really their home away from home, too. In the meantime they were renovating a trailer they were fixing up out in the hills. They didn't need a son and Raymond was around all the time.

He didn't smoke, listened to all kinds of music, usually hard rock, constantly lunched on self-made ham sandwiches, with a jar of pickles, and worked at a leisurely pace.

He hailed from somewhere in Michigan. Never said much about his youth. Would talk about too many things when he pinned you down in conversation. He'd go on about his journals, his weird and perverse attempts at poetry, or what he called his own type of new literature. He would sketch little caricatures all about the Gallery, mostly near the wall where the phone was. A note about the phone: it was once white. Underneath its years of grime from iron dust and grease and ketchup smears and mouthfuls of smoke, was its original shell, now cracked, but miraculously keeping its guts of electricity functioning.

Raymond did the faces of everyone at work. None too well, either. Never himself, and no one knows why. His favorite writer was Lewis Carroll. Sometimes he brought in his books, loaned from the library, and books on photography most usually dedicated to the subject of the nude. The man was starved for affection even though he had a girlfriend.

She was a big woman of Swedish-Irish decent who sometimes moonlighted for the Gallery as a book-keeper, and who always was in between lousy, low-pay jobs. Her name was Anne. She was a clean freak, thus her visits to the Gallery were far and in between.

When she did show up, she was quite nice to everyone. Big smiles and ample gossip. She talked of the goings-on of the small town she lived in. These stories involved infidelity, drunkenness, tragedy, heartbreak, and resolution. And she regularly tried to pawn off her stock of natural, health conscious, green cleaning supplies. She was sort of a rep for a local company, toting in these expensive products made by hippies gone bourgeois, to sell to the business at cut rate prices. Out of pity Nora bought a few and kept them under the sink of the bathroom, so no one would ever discover such a transaction of folly.

Once, the happy couple of Raymond and Anne decided to have a dinner party to show off the new house they had just rented. Three bedrooms, a porch, a cellar, big kitchen, right in the midst of the town (678 population) for only two hundred and fifty dollars a month. The reason why humans continue to populate the Midwest is obvious. It's called rent.

The carpets of the first floor level had been just cleaned. The orange lawn of the main room was brilliant; the sea green of the hall was luxurious. Raymond's paintings hung on every available inch of wall space. Anne put out bowls of pretzels and nuts as appetizers. There was a bouquet of prairie wildflowers adorning a coffee table varnished, by the smell of it, a day hence.

Three of the nine people invited came. A tumultuous downpour broke half an hour before the get-together. When the first guest came in, Pablo, Anne almost fainted at the wet footprints he left in the carpet, but she composed herself while fixing her hair in the tiny half-bathroom off of the kitchen.

Mikey came in next, toting dope smoking paraphernalia, and started to light up at his presumed seat at the dinner table. Much to the chagrin of Anne, Raymond joined him, and within minutes, the house smelled of a skunk farm. Dana arrived shortly after and remarked that the place smelled as sweet as highway ditch in the height of summer.

Anne asked everyone to sit down, put on an LP of Nina Simone, and brought out from the oven the main dish: roasted pheasant. Raymond popped open the bottle of California rouge. Mikey was especially hungry so he asked to be passed the cold corn salad.

When Raymond sat down, his knees jolted the table, which spilled the bottle of wine all over it, then, as he was getting up to make amends for the mess, hit his head on the overhung light fixture which rained down a flurry of dried up insects, mostly moths and gnats.

Anne turned red. Then she began to almost cry.

The rain outside was coming down in sheets. Dana didn't mind the spice of dried bugs on her portion of the pheasant and began eating it, after scraping them off with her knife, joking about the mysterious, but very good indeed, flavoring. Anne bolted up out of her chair and ran upstairs to the sound of a slamming door.

Party that had begun was over. The three of them finished the food, opened up another bottle of wine, this time white, and a six pack appeared from the cellar. A steady drip of water had begun to squeeze its way through the crack on the ceiling in the kitchen so Raymond promptly put the empty mashed potato pan underneath. Nora, Mikey, and Raymond went to sit on the porch since they were getting wet indoors anyway, turned up the volume of the record player, and set their sights on smoking the rest of the dope until only its dust and a few seeds remained.

Dana and Mikey apologized for the stream of events, the lack of others, etcetera, but Raymond shrugged it off, rationalizing that Anne could miss a few meals for the better. They called for her to come down; she said she would in a minute.

Mikey, on a whim of flighty intoxication, told Raymond that his pictures were awful pretty—the still lives of medicinal plants, the rural land forms, the sheet, and the portraits of locals, but wondered out loud why there weren't any nudes.

Raymond eased himself back into his iron rocking chair and attempted thought. He said, well, that, it was a case of, well, never meeting a model (meaning a woman) with a body of a model (meaning perfect) who would get to know me well enough to feel comfortable enough to disrobe in front of me. While he said this he was looking at Dana's heels, exposed by her clogs.

He said his dream was to find just such a perfect female, classic body-caring mind-intelligent and loving, not to have as a lover, but as a friend, a partner in the artistic process, as he put it, and he would capture her essence in a singular nude study that he would never show to the public, but just keep in his studio, his own personal Galatea, as a reminder of what?: time, death, the joy of the physical. For all the parties Raymond went to, and all the bars, and all the art shows and vernissages, it was impossible for him to find this a priori woman concealed in so many different bodies layered in so many layers of confusing clothes.

The Dream of the Country

To have more trees. In every ditch, each muddy plain, every valley, near the lips of every crick, in the hollows measured by shelves of stacked limestone, on sides and tops of hills, near fence posts of rotten standing wood, in fields and around their edges, in the basements of abandoned houses, under water tanks that resemble UFOs, within the spaces of already clogged, overgrown woods, more trees.

Maples, oak, dwarf junipers, birches, pines, poplars, cedars, crabapple, more oaks, and even junipers.

To be gently undulating rows of hills, like snakes digesting decent meals, covered in green and absconding the jungles of wildlife underneath. Red foxes with white plumes of tails, beavers with their fish-like paddles constructing pyramids of driftwood and fresh tree trunk, wood rats the enemies of families of quail, crazy stupid pheasants who in a different life would be road runners, the mythical horses of deer, legions of insects with and without carapaces, stinging biting creatures of many colors and sizes penetrating the nectar of poisonous plants, penetrating husks of feces. Penetrating animal and human skin.

Only inlet to this world, this world within the world, through paths of river, stream, and creek, themselves undulating in a natural journey to the sea. Slowly, wavelessly moving in one direction, carrying seeds of trees and wild flower and plant life, spores of mushroom, dead fish and birds, drowned men and women who should have known better, geodes and smooth river rock tumbling on the bottom.

Marshes with their keepers of raccoons, loudly alive with the chirp of too many frogs, and in the summer, the insanity of cicadas (little red eyes seeing). Pond snakes, crawdads wondering what it would be like to be a lobster, zebra clams going about their own business. Bones of the unlucky, or simply finished, being polished and assumed by water, to be spat out on a sandy bank and used as something by another form of life, like a tool, or decoration, a symbol for the final destination of the flow.

Great plains of grass that move like lakes in the wind. Containing birds' nests and their sweet treasures of speckled eggs, hives of bees and hornets hidden away from the electric eyes of hawks, ever circling, and diving like thrown knives, overhead.

Clouds, waiting to burst, accumulating on the horizon, bowls of cream curdling. Mid-afternoon. Cumulus, floating as newly hatched birds, confident with flight, waiting to disperse in red rays of sunset, then deep magenta, then dark blue, then obsidian. Stars wound into patterns, outlines of nothing in particular. The dream of the country, to exist another day.

The Dream of James

He didn't speak much, but when James Engleterre did say some-
thing, is was usually this: "I just want to be normal." For him,
it was not an unusual request. He was the workhorse of the Gallery,
a man of large breadth. Thick fingers and thick arms connected to a
thick body that was topped off with a thick pony-tail hanging from
a relatively large head. He enjoyed exercising his body more than his
mind, although he did read a lot, usually about medieval times. About
knights and chivalry and the imaginary conquests of old Europe.

He was a crusader of manual labor who took on the dirty work of
the business such as breaking apart molds, constructing new machines
and keeping the old ones running, lifting excruciating pounds of metal,
moving equipment from one place to another while cursing loudly.
His invectives would resound through the morning-empty building.
He had worked there the longest and always talked about leaving to
get a real job in a real factory so he wouldn't have to torture himself in
a place where one had to spend as much time making things work as
making the things themselves. His quotidian unhappiness made him
happy and this, in turn, infuriated him.

He was divorced from a lovely little woman with a full head of
blonde hair. She worked at the ice cream shop near the highway and
James would drop by there at least once a week to get free eats. They
served hot dogs and hamburgers and cold salami sandwiches because
the farmer that owned it had a lot of land with milk and meat cattle
grazing it. No one knew where the salami came from.

It was as obvious as sin that James still loved his ex and the reasons
why he did and the reasons why she left him. He was a brute but a
lovable one and proved this by showing up at the Gallery with a bag
of week old pretzels and a jar of mustard that she gave him out of pity
or maybe just to keep him away for another stretch of time. He would
offer them around the table at lunch saying that they were *damn* good
pretzels, dip one into the jar, and eat it whole. They were little chewy
things without salt and slid down the throat easily.

James had a habit of working like a dog in the morning and mid-afternoon so he could leave work early and apply for other jobs. It was his idea to get a job delivering mail because it paid well and one was left alone during the day. He envisioned himself driving an old rickety mail jeep down dusty gravel roads while listening to the a.m. radio with a six pack of beer under the seat. Surrounded by fields empty with horses and goats and cows with monotony broken every mile or so by a farmhouse, tractors and machinery lined up on mud driveways, a laundry line dancing with a household of clothes, and a little barn shaped mailbox waiting for a visit.

He wasn't an irrational man. He couldn't stand the way the Gallery ran, the day to day struggle that tore away at his nerves was what made him raw. The whimsical schedules for getting things done that Rex, the head of the Gallery, made, and the way he went about telling James what needed to be done, if he had the time, or if he could, was in the eyes of James, a class in belittlement. Big men don't like to be made small.

Most of the time James would shake off the shit Rex said to him with a shrug and a few choice phrases under his breath. Sometimes he would go out back into the piles of rusting scrap metal, wearing a pair of plastic goggles, and break old radiators apart to release some of his, and the metal's, inherit tension. Sometimes it was so bad that he had to, after throwing a rubber-headed mallet across the shop at a piece of sheet metal or some such resonant target, leave. Many a time in the dreary part of the afternoon when lunch is settling into the gut and the artists got back to what they were doing, except at a slower pace, the sound of first something being thrown, then the slamming of a car door, then acceleration, could be heard. Everybody knew it was James having another one of his days. He would be expected to come in the next morning a little later than usual, but with no malice on his tongue, and perhaps after drinking the night away, no memory of the previous day's disgruntle.

When he could get the business work of the shop done, like making molds for barn door hinges or mufflers for now extinct tractors, he worked on his own projects. Invariably, they were weapons. Spear tips, sword handles, iron duplicates of pioneer tools used for skinning deer, and even once, he made a mace. He hadn't sharpened the spikes on the mace yet, which made everyone feel a bit more reassured, especially Rex. Even dull, the thing could have done serious damage to anything that came in between it and James' swinging arm. He kept it on a wooden shelf above his work station. It was sort of his symbol and an omen for what might happen if he was pushed too far. James rarely ever held his tools of destruction in a threatening manner, rather, he handled them delicately, giving them beautiful bright finishes and polishing them after they were ground and sanded and threaded to precision. Tools of destruction, his pride and joy.

The periodic times his car would break down forced James into asking for the favor of a ride into or from work. One thing that kept the Gallery together more than forcing its participants to leave was the desperately low wages working there offered. Thus, missing a day of work was equal to missing a day's meals. It was crucial to suffer the misery of another long hard day because it was crucial to remain alive.

When he was in the car with someone else, he would really open up. It was the speed that did it and the movement on the quiet roads that led him to talk about his wild youthful days of drunk driving, stealing DeKalb corn signs, hanging around the restaurant where liquor was served to get customers to by them pitchers, and the glorious isolated past of events that took place to the audience of non-caring, swaying in the wind, cornfields.

One danger of driving into the town each morning was falling back asleep. A fog would envelop the shallow valleys, not much traffic, the only voice a drone of the man reading a book on the radio. But this was impossible with James in the passenger seat because he would rant on about how wonderful and maybe even happy his life was before he got stuck in the rut of his job and lonely life with not much to look forward to except the next drinking occasion or hope of a big money making project with a local archeologist from the university who wanted to reproduce a tool for sale at little craft shows that bloomed all throughout the country come spring and the endless hard to breathe in summer months.

Monday was James' favorite day for it was payday. Throughout the morning, clipboards that hung on the office wall were removed to be pondered over, which usually took a self-indulgent hour of figuring, scamming hours worked so they would fit into a forty hour total, each hour meticulously notated with a travail accomplished, or at least attempted, then turned into Beth the secretary who would in turn figure out the taxes and write each worker a check. James was always the first to come into work on Monday and assiduously complete his worksheet, get his check and briskly walk to the bank on the corner to first, cash it to gain money for lunch, and secondly, get a free bag of popcorn that the bank offered. When he returned to the Gallery, he would offer a half-eaten white paper bag to anyone who wanted to share it by putting it on the office desk and the place, for the rest of the day, would smell like a country fair.

One Monday when Rex was in one of his anti-James moods, mostly because he hated any form of consistency, such as James' penchant for getting paid but not, in his opinion, beginning the day's work which was of the utmost importance, this day it being hammering edition numbers into the iron underbellies of a series of cooperatively owned alligator sculptures so they then could be painted lake-green and shipped to Florida. So Rex asked James to do the Gallery a favor by depositing a check.

On the check that Rex concealed in an envelope were written the words: "This is a hold-up. Put the money in a bag. Do it quiet like." Every fifth or so letter was spelled backwards—funny like a child would write it so the recipient would know it was a joke. Not knowing of the wicked intent, James agreed to take it to the bank with his prized check of seven hundred and something dollars, fisted the envelope, stuffed it in his shirt pocket without even looking at it or thinking about it, and left the Gallery leaving the bell bolted to the door loudly jingling.

James took the long way to the bank, past the antique stores trying their sleepiest to open their roll-shaded doors. The hardware store was already open with farmers inside chatting about the month's weather and possibility and impossibilities of things needing to be done. They wore knee-high boots covered with mud and manure and nodded to

James because they knew him by his looks. He was dirty, as soiled in appearance as they were, yet more so because he did work incomprehensible to them. Work in dust and grease and metal but which never resulted in anything they could fathom. The community consisted mostly of farmers who would never dare set foot in the Gallery to peer into the strange pictureless pictures framed on the walls, or the lumps of all that bronze wasted into shapes of humans doing who knows what, but sometimes when they needed something to be welded back together, like a trailer hitch, they would appear at the back door, ask Rex to do it, and anxiously look at the others who were always too busy to be bothered.

When James passed the bakery, he couldn't hardly stand the smell of donuts being fried and had to turn his head away from the window because he was so hungry and couldn't wait to cash his earnings. In his head he was making out a breakfast list which included a cinnamon roll, two long-johns, and two pints of milk, with a straw. He took the alley behind Main Street to see if any of the businesses were throwing anything of value away. There was a broken-looking television set, a bunch of two by fours, a rain-stained lampshade, and an old tin oil burner used for heating up rooms. He made a mental note to pass by again after hours on his way out of town to maybe scavenge.

He had to wait five minutes for the bank to officially open. For some reason, the bank had a large wooden representation of a boat over its door. He could hear the popcorn machine warming up and the first sputtering of kernels being popped. It really was going to be a good day.

A smallish pig-faced man unlocked the doors and James was the first one in, followed by some older women, an Amish, a few stray leaves. The bank was ready to do business, a radio was turned onto country music in the back, and a telephone rang from somewhere above. The boat bank was in the process of getting its first cash machine and some local carpenters appeared to continue the work of creating a space for it. They worked in the entrance fit for only a few people at a time, so they had to either enter the bank or leave it to let people pass through. There was really no need for the modern convenience especially since a person wouldn't be able to access the robotic device after bank hours anyway and there were never any long lines, even on Friday afternoons because farmers had no set hours and made no money anyway, yet it was something new fangled and the popcorn machine wasn't bringing them in anymore.

Out of chivalry, James let the women step ahead of him. They were sure to thank him in between talking non-stop about the price of groceries while he stood behind them listening. They left the bank smiling.

When James handed over the envelope from his pocket and his paycheck, the teller looked at him, looked back down at the paper from the envelope, and hit the alarm button under the counter. The doors immediately locked and everyone inside hit the floor. James cursed loudly not knowing what was happening and within moments, a police car pulled up in front of the bank.

The cops megaphoned that no one inside should move, that the doors were going to be unlocked, that they were coming in. James was laying on the floor trembling with his paycheck in between his teeth and sweat beading on his forehead. The cops, two of them, cautiously entered the building, stepping over the carpenters and their spilled tools, and looked at the bank manager who, in a graceful movement of arm and index finger, pointed at James' place on the floor. They picked him up and hauled him out. He said nothing, thinking that perhaps his wife was sore about another missed alimony payment or some such trifle. He knew one of the officers: a drinking and pool playing buddy of his, Dale Robbins. The other officer read him his rights in the car, and James remained silent. They explained about the note. James said he'd call Rex from the station, a few blocks from the Gallery with his one allotted phone call. He said that he was glad to be momentarily incarcerated because he was going to kill Rex. Kill him painfully and slowly.

When the chief of police saw the check with Rex's scrawling on it, he knew it was a stupid joke, so they didn't lock James up in one of the two cells. He asked James what he did to deserve a prank like this. No response. James was looking at his still uncashed paycheck which was smeared indecipherable by teeth marks and saliva. The police station was housed in a former gas station, nothing on the walls except a tool calendar. There was a telephone, a CB, a coffee machine. It turned out that Henry Vinton heard the bank's alarm go off while he was talking to a friend at the butcher's and tractored himself up to the station to let the authorities know.

James crumpled up the paper, threw it to the floor, bit his lower lip, and began biting his fingernails and swallowing them because he was so hungry. Under his breath he whispered, I'm going get another job I'm going to get another job tomorrow.

James was fully aware that his dream was to have a dream.

The Dream of Nora

Rumor had it that Nora had always been an enigma of herself. There were pictures taped to the wall of herself in former incarnations. She kept a running billboard of her life in the office, on a wall parallel to the door, so customers wouldn't be invited to look at it, unless they were real curious and moved about the room. She had always been, for lack of a better word, mythical.

Her progression in the last twelve or so years could be gauged. Her hair was light auburn, worn short, except for a pony tail running down from the top of her head, down the side of her face, and resting, in one picture, in the crease of her breasts. Of Norwegian, or Swedish, or Latvian, or Danish ancestry, she once said, and maybe she changed the story form time to time. Nevertheless, she was embarrassingly white, with crisp grey eyes, now straight auburn hair loosely twisted into a braid and usually tucked under one of her innumerable queer hats. Train engineer, beret, stocking (for sleeping), straw field, Polish riding, Stetson, Louisiana pith, dock workers black cap—she had, and wore, them all.

The big secret, a secret because it went wholly unacknowledged, but was well known, was the fact that it was Nora's creations, her sculptures of mainly animals that kept the Gallery running. She had hundreds of orders for her work, mostly small bronze representations of toads, deer, bison, the natural life that represented the wildlife of the nature of the region. They were small enough to be purchasable by the public, usually ranging in the hundred to two hundred dollar range, could be cranked out quickly, didn't utilize much costly bronze, and were in high demand. These small, remarkably beautiful things were used, from customer feedback, from paper weights to garden decorations to bookends. People loved them because they were just that, small and accurate, finely patina-ed works of art.

Her forté was creating the original pieces, then letting the other artists take over the factory line process of mass producing them. In that juncture of will, desire, and follow through, a problem arose. After the initial burst of inspiration it took to create a fawn scratching its ear a moment before falling in its awkwardness– the moment forever frozen in bronze– it was a dreary process to organize and carry out the manufacturing of four hundred of the same for some knick-knack store in South Bend, Indiana.

Thusly, each morning Nora would arise her own work weary body, drain three cups of Japanese tea, put on a tape of Patsy Cline, and slowly, ever so slowly, after feeding her three dogs who also lived at the Gallery, then feeding and taking care of Wellington, a European Starling she had rescued from abandonment, who lived in a cage, sang to his favorite music, drank beer, and ate fried chicken, she would then attempt to muster the enthusiasm of the other workers to get her endless march of wildlife into the wax, then ceramic shell, then molten metal, finishing, then patina stage. Not to forget the paperwork and shipping of the little creatures tucked lovingly into nests of shredded newspaper and cellophane tape. Reluctant as God, her fun was in the creating, but not the running of her offsprings' lives.

Yet her work, and occasional initiative, provided the income and busywork for the Gallery to hire and pay the other artists, who dealt most of the time with her work, so they, in turn, could use the equipment of the Gallery for the pursuit of their own artworks, in the hopes of gaining the kind of following Nora had for hers.

She was on the teetering verge of success and this bred resentment.

But Nora was a dreamer and spent most of her time doing that. Strolling the town and the bordering woods, feeding other peoples' horses grass and weed flowers she gleaned from big, empty, abandoned fields, talking to the woman who owned the natural health food store (for hours), launching her theories about why some animals acted one way or another, like why the bark of a fox sounds like a screaming woman, basically doing anything to stay on the periphery of actually doing the work that stood before her. Each and every drawn out day.

She took care of things and took pleasure doing so. She lived with Rex in both the loft in the back of the gallery, separated from the work areas by a huge sliding white slab of drywall with rope handle attached, and in their mobile home complex they both had begun assembling on some farmland out in the hollows. She cooked meals of rabbit stew, leg of lamb, and sometimes, by request of Pablo only, cow's tongue. She'd jump at the chance to warm up a bowl of any of the above and share it at lunch or closing time. She was nice like that.

The day she had to take care of Wilamette was one of the worst days in her recent memory. She'd gone through an extra long procrastination in the morning, having made cups of tea for everyone coming in that day, even one for Raymond at his entrance of 10:48 am, and began telling and re-telling the story of the reason why she believed in ghosts.

It happened in Louisiana, on a farm, or more specifically, in the marsh just beyond the wooden fences of her father's attempt at starting a farm, the land, grazing cattle, goats, and all. She said it was just about at nightfall, when she and her sister were through playing dolls in their favorite-most weeping willow. The tree you could climb almost to the very top of to get a view of the surrounding lowlands and the farmhouse built upon a muddy running creek that meandered, died out, and somehow magically started up again, cutting through domes of loam and carrying in its current the tiny black dots of bugs' eggs.

She and her sis had muddied their own clothes in the ritualistic behaviors that little girls will partake in– mindlessly, instinctively, such as cutting the follicles of yarn off the dolls heads and planting the red and yellow bundle near the base of the willow in hopes that it would grow a new kind of tree or bush. After they'd done this, and lost two of the tea cups of their newly bought plastic tea time set, they heard strange crackling noises off in the distance, coming somewhere within the watery muck of the marsh, really more of a swamp, even though it was northern Louisiana and not actual delta land, a place they had been forbidden to ever go for fear of drowning or getting stuck in quick sand that was so lethal their father called it fast sand.

When two shining orbs calmly made way through, in and out of, and around the brambly weeds and low-lying bushes, then sort of just stopped and hung there, in plain air, pulsating and glowing like fireflies incapable of turning off, the girls screamed, and ran.

What Nora remembers distinctly is running faster than she ever ran in her life, before then or after, with one of the bald dolls clutched in her arm, and the leg of the other doll between her arm and ribcage, and for one second, turning her head to see the two bulbs of light approach the wooden fence, and instead of going through its broadly spaced beams, up and over it ever so gracefully, then float to the big metallic trunk of the willow, and just as she and her sister had done a countless number of boring afternoons, shimmy up the tree and disappear into its nether worldly, uppermost branches.

First thing shot back at her, inevitably, when she told this true to life account, no one doubted her perception at the least, was the reply: swamp gas. But she always denied the accusation with a vigorous sweeping of the head in the almost universal movement of negation, nope, no way. Couldn't have been. She had the same very reaction to "heat lightning". Her rationalization being that experience had lead her to the observation of both of those natural occurrences and what she saw was neither. We all have our ghosts. Nora had hers. They were probably just that. Friendly ghosts taking a stroll one humid landlocked night, with only the vague promise of an ocean in that tepid old pool that hid the bones of whom?

This morning she had a definite plan to carry out her work plan and nothing but her own meandering thoughts could prevent her. Those tangents and riffs of thinking little things and doing odd bits of other seemingly useless activities, such as trimming the bird's toenails, were all part of the meditative process. She woke Wilamette up from a deep, drooly slumber, putting her red body harness on. The dog was sort of a barely living miracle—a sixteen year old Great Dane, grey in color, and hardly able to walk more than a half mile before collapsing in weary sleep the remainder of the day. Nora got her up early this morning, tempting her strength and vigor with a plastic grocery bag filled with sheep brains.

She took her out across the field which was adjacent to the Gallery, in plain yawning view of the men working in the wax pouring room, and paused only to regard a giant dead tree branch bonfire the city workers had assembled and lit in the gully near Vinton's place. The city workers held cans of Budweiser behind their backs, as to not cause attention to themselves, as they too watched the flames reach a three storey level. Nora thought it a sacrificial fire honoring the nothing itself that took place within the town each day. She passed by the men murmuring something, or singing, couldn't tell from the Gallery window, as the men themselves said something to, or about her, and kind of waved, as she and the huge limping dog, passed by.

Nora hee-hoed Vinton's two quarter horses out on the land grazing as she went by his place. Didn't stop to offer them any grass, which they thought strange, a look in their eyes, the stillness of their heads, their not-chewing mouths indicated that something was up.

She and the dog walked down the mud road leading to Vinton's farm fields, still about elbow low with new corn growing and dancing slowly in the rays of bright sun. She got to a grassy area where a few killdeer were hiding out, and took off with their silly, wild cries, at the sound of footfall and the smell of matted fur.

She got down on her knees, patted Wilamette lovingly all about her head and long twisted body, then unrolled the package of sheep brains on the grass in front of the dog. Wilamette lustily ate at the bloody mess, not thinking a thing, and happy, as food is paradise for hungry beasts. Nora stood up, slowly, and watched her beloved chow down.

Amidst the slobber and growling noises the dog had been used to making at meal time, Nora unwrapped Rex's .38 from a shammy. She pumped three shots, as not to screw up, through the dog's head, and safely into the deep soil just under it.

She would return and hour and a half later, with a shovel, to bury Wilamette properly, after she had cried, with warm hot tears soaking into the collar of her dirty work shirt. Nora knew how to take care of things.

The dream of Nora was one that ceaselessly continued.

The Dream of Rex

Rex was as complex as a carbohydrate, and burned as much energy. Constantly. If he wasn't working at any given moment, he was preparing to work, which is pre-work work, so it's work anyway. The man was professionally nervous. If Nora was the source of the Gallery, Rex, with his thousands of sculptures, and ideas that took the form of sculpture, was its genius.

Like a true artist, the only worthwhile kind to know, nothing much was known about him. That is, nothing much was revealed. He was a local boy—local in the sense that he was from a small town about a hundred and twenty miles north of from where he established his business, went to the university none too far away where he learned his craft, had a falling out with his mentor that he sometimes alluded to without including the details, and never lived anywhere else but his home state. He was a veteran traveler of the arts and crafts scene: fairs in tourists towns all around the country, conferences on the process of bronze and iron melting (technical, boring foundry stuff as he referred to it), had an isolationist's character, and survived off a large sum of dough he once received as an heir, but mostly, he lived off his deranged wits.

He had the face of what's best described as an Antagonist. Red hair cut short, as if he did it himself with scissors, freckles, a nose of a Baron's. As the self-assumed boss, he ran things tight, complained about the artists that he himself hired, except for Pablo, and on the hour tried to influence anyone within his proximity to work on his projects, always without the least concern for his or anyone else's safety or well-being. He'd have you clean out old corn-coaters full of toxic waste, with a steel brush and a pair of dish washing gloves, and think nothing about it. He'd arc weld bits of metal together in an attempt to make a new tool, wearing sunglasses and a ripped t-shirt. His care was one and one only: to get the next thing done.

Rex made things. Bottle openers in relief portraits of Elvis, Ghandhi, Nixon. Skulls of famous Neanderthals with added gold teeth.

Bronze dinosaurs capturing and eating planes. Collector's items before they were even finished. He once did a bronze sculpture of Durer's rhinoceros that was an exact three dimensional reproduction, weighed a couple of hundred pounds, and was sold before it was finished. To survive, he took on commissions of governmental art, mostly for the state, and did a competent job with those. His preference was to make useless items like self-portraits as a light bulb, real looking donuts which were slightly stale, crafted out of iron, and sell them to whoever would buy, or to little stores. Unfortunately, most of the folks who ventured into the gallery were so awestruck at the amount of queer little things he produced that they couldn't choose one. And he had to loft big price tags on them because so few actually sold, at least locally, so there was a viscious cycle of a stalled market spun around his project. Only a hand-countable amount of galleries on the East coast dared, and had enough financial backing, to purchase from his catalogue. If Rex was an ornery fellow, at least what he made was irresistible.

Out of the hatchback of a '76 Ford Pinto (yes, the model with an exploding rear end) Rex crafted a makeshift sandblaster. Not really makeshift since it had been in use for the last eight years, functioning half heartedly, liable to not work more than it worked, and just an overall pain to use. He replaced the window of the car's, now machine's, viewing cage with a sheet of Teflon. It would automatically and logically become covered with mite-sized scratches from the flying particles of sand within hours of use, thus making the blasting of bronze pieces within it a game of guess work and intuition. Basically, one couldn't see the object one was attempting to finish, and blasting away bright white kernels of dried ceramic shell from a golden bronze representation of a horned toad, realistic to each and every scale on its thorny back, became a process of intense futility. Adding to the fact that the worker had to wear a rubber head cover that also was concocted by Rex and looked like a primitive diving helmet, and underneath that, protective eyeglasses which would inevitably fog up with the wearer's own desperate breath, a relatively simple job of squirting a fast moving stream of sand onto a hand-held object became similar to driving down the highway, in rush hour with a windshield covered in a sheet of blinding ice. So went apprenticeship under the tutelage of Rex.

After hiring a new farm boy (an Amish kid eagerly desiring to enter the secular world) Rex had him work on a special project. He took the young man out into the backyard of the Gallery. There, he had him suit up in an outer space get up consisting of the regulation pads of a National League catcher: stomach and chest pad, knee and shin pads, catcher's mask embellished with a plastic inner shield that did not allow for any flow of oxygen until it was removed, leather welding gloves, and a sledgehammer. The kid's job for the morning was to break apart old iron radiators, of which there was a piled up stock of about thirty or so, towards the goal of using the junk metal in an iron meltdown and eventually, pour. This required that each radiator, ancient dinosaurs of things, be broken, literally smashed down into pieces measuring four by four inches.

At first the yokel, as the others referred to him, had at it with the spirit of an unbroken horse. It was actually kind of fun to destroy things, to go all out on inanimate objects clad in the armor of a samurai warrior. After a half an hour, when the sweat from his forehead began obscuring his vision, and shrapnel began pinching at the parts of his body where the padding didn't overlap (bend in the arm, neck, ankles), and the Babel-like tower of rusty radiators began to barely diminish and in fact, in the dizziness caused by over extension and lack of oxygen, seem to grow, to tower above and even begin to slowly undulate and reveal patterns of symbols in its alembic of shorn away parts. Didn't that piece over there look like an old wheelchair, and that accumulation look like the tools of a civil war surgeon—there was a final loud thud two hours and twelve minutes into the venture. He had collapsed.

Pablo was the first to run out to the scene and throw his giant-sized plastic mug of iced-tea, including the ice cubes, onto the fallen drone. Nora tore away his mask and smartly began giving him CPR, really an inspiring sight to see—the fluidity of her body in action like it rarely ever was anymore, her leaping and crouching above the poor kid, plastering her mouth upon his, her copious breasts spilling out of the top of her buttoned shirt onto his neck, while infusing him with her hot morning breath. When he responded, after barely thirty seconds, he did so by grabbing her waist and buttocks, and returning the charitable gesture with as much force as he was previously hacking away at metal, to the surprise, then applause, of the other workers (unfortunately it was morning and hardly any one was there to see the spectacle), as Nora burst out laughing so hard and blushing so red that it squeezed tears out of the far corners of her eyes.

Apparently the boy wasn't so Amish after all.

Not possible to not hate him, in some way near or even remotely, Rex did start things going. He put it into motion, though the results would usually be destruction, but at least real beauty in its trajectory of demise.

One of his habits was to round up bored looking workers at the Gallery, around 2:30 p.m., when there really was nothing to do, the sun high in the sky, the humidity secretly rolling in from the banks of burbling rivers, the worst time of the day for feeling useful. Rex would parade through the wax room, enlivened by his lunch of peanut butter and jelly sandwiches, a beer (or three), and attempt to enlist forces, as he said it, to do some work, off the books for his own private projects such as dry-walling his studio apartment, which was more of a living-shed, in the back of the Gallery's air hanger like accumulation of attached buildings.

A list of odd jobs, according to Rex's divine plans, should suffice in explicating the long array of futile hours that could be wasted away. Repairing the engine of the five ton forklift that hadn't moved from its centrally located position in the sand molding area for six and one half years. Clean-up of any room, including the removal of stratums of dust, really years and years of iron fillings. Endless, Sisyphusian iron breakdown assuring the volunteer physical exhaustion and oftentimes mental thrown in to boot. Organization and inventory-ing of the hundreds of bronze and iron poured sculptures of Rex that were awaiting, first, an order, and secondly, hours of finishing time. These were heaped into pyramid shapes all about the largest single area in the Gallery, the pouring room, and thus covered in years of ash and dust. Some of these works were even sprouting moss. Domicile-oriented jobs such as repairing his two and a half mile driveway that led to his farmhouse, that he was in the process of moving out of, but wanted to repair so he could better haul out his stuff into a mobile home-like complex of lean-tos that he had amassed on a large chunk of land he somehow managed to wrangle under his name using the asset of the Gallery itself.

Rex didn't like bourbon. This is something Pablo found out, early one freezing morning, the day after Rex was evicted from his farmhouse that he'd lived in for eight some years. Probably he was kicked out due to the fact that he never not once cleaned the place, that the carpet on the floors became more of a large, room-to-room blanket of dog hair, the bathroom toilet completely rusted a brilliant red hue, the windows opaque, the basement and attic so cluttered with things that they were unidentifiable under cloaks of dust and grime.

He was in a spot. Pablo was the first to come into the Gallery that morning, so Rex pleaded for his assistance, in his characteristic whiny voice, to begin moving his stuff from the house into the back of the business. He had nowhere else to go. The temperature was near twenty-eight degrees without the bite of wind. Pablo agreed to help. But first he went back into the old back office, found the hidden bottle of bourbon, filled his canteen with half water, half spirits, buttoned up his overshirt, and left with Rex in the pick-up.

Rex wouldn't drink any of the stuff, assigning his distaste for it due to a night of overuse, about twenty years back. He did find an old butt in the loaded ashtray, and lit up by taking a blue tip from his front pocket and flicking it aflame with his grimy fingernail. Pablo sipped at his canteen and hummed to the crackling song on the radio. A.M.

First they got the important stuff, the necessities. Bed, once-white refrigerator, sofa, a box of pots and pans. They stacked it in just that order and bungee-corded it steady.

About half way back to the Gallery, they barely heard a chiming, like bells ringing, behind them, distanced. The box of pots and pans had taken flight. Rex said *Sheeeet, mother of mercy*, laid on the brakes, and turned the truck around. Pablo crooked his neck backwards, then forwards, to see the mess. He thought to himself: yet another normal outing with the Boss.

Ever since that day, and there were many more trips and many more bungled loads, Rex had lived at least part-time in the business he began. Eight months after his move, he bought acres of land, found a mostly dilapidated mobile home at an auction, traded the owner some scrap aluminum siding for it, and commenced to build a kingdom on earth in the fields and hills three and a half miles away from his work.

The mobile home idea was one of Rex's ideas for a sculpture come true. On a hillcrest he deposited the long rectangle, complete with wood paneled walls and orange linoleum in the kitchen. Rex rigged up a sump pump to the well on the property to get a flow of water into the shell of a place. Behind where it laid, there were abandoned beehives that he enlarged and used as dog houses for his animals. He fenced in part of the surrounding prairie to make a yard. He made an entry way to the yard, a tall gate of sorts, constructed out of deer bones he found on the land. He built a bonfire pit out front.

Some nights, from the gravel road that passed by the property, passing farmers would see the tops of the trees up on the hill. Rex would be out there, drinking the cheapest canned beer he could buy, and adding on. Occasionally, after work, he'd try to wrangle the late stayers to come out to the estate, as he called it, tempting them with a meal of fire cooked knackwurst and generic beer.

The dream of Rex was a long, complex one, really unfathomable, but had something to do with tools, disjunctive parts welded together, the freedom of the imagination to create at will, to create something out of what other people considered junk. But as in a nightmare, his creations became to be regarded as simply more junk. The dream of Rex was an impossible one, in the end. It was a dream to create a world of his own device within the outer world of hum-drumness, a world of endless possibility, peopled with objects of an undeniable author, living signatures of things that worked until they needed to be attended to, and in the attending to the broken down, a paradigm of life in this other world, seemed to function in its malfunctioning. Death to Rex was not a fear, but a distaste for the horror of inaction, of stasis. Rex said it best when Pablo asked him why he loved so much to burn things. His reply: to see what ashes make.

121

The Dream of Pablo

Logically, one is led to Pablo. It is because he is the wellsource, that is, in the fishbowl of hungry artists. He came from San An-tone, was a mixture of Spanish cowboy, Amerindian, and wide-eyed optimistic American labeled as Hispanic. It was more than possible that his roots, especially his spiritual roots, came from Franco-Spaniard cowboys of the Camargue region of southern France. He painted portraits, many times, in charcoal and pastel too, as just such a figure.

He bled sweat when he worked and worked his ass off. Ten to twelve hour days. He traveled the country in art shows, always eager to meet those rare, usually doctors and lawyers these days, few folks who had a taste for private collections of art. A black book the size of a bible he kept with him at all times holding the names and address of galleries (big time) in New York, St. Louis, Kansas City, Denver, Phoenix, that had bought or at one time displayed his sculptures. He made big things.

A Gulf stream mermaid, harlequins in mocking positions, nudes of men and women he knew. He wasn't notorious for sleeping with his models, and he kept these secretive narratives within the fields of his compositions. Many early paintings in the realistic mode, but with Southwestern colors, vibrancy. Most of his female nudes tilted their heads away from the viewer, anonymous, known only by physical characteristics, the contours of their bodies.

Still lives of boxes of razor blades, collections of burnt candle stubs, shelves of acrylics; never landscapes, or exteriorizations of anything other than the reflecting tain of his mind.

He was committed to living out a long tenure of his life at the Gallery. He had invested tens of thousands into bronze, made all that metal into sculptures, had sold half of them, and at least a quarter had interested collectors enough for Pablo to gain their following, if not a promise to buy. The catch to this seemingly success story lies within his talents. Since he was the most useful and skilled among the artists, the Gallery needed his abilities to finish its contracts with the real world. Most of the clientele would by habit ask for Pablo to head and supervise their projects and this, though a great compliment, left him no time to complete his own work. He became the afterhours jockey, even more so than Rex. He became that lonely guy in the desolate scenes of Hopper's paintings—all that was needed was a late drive by the Gallery, on any night, and there'd be a few light bulbs burning, and the solitary music of Pablo hammering away at his craft.

Half of his life was an interminable road movie. He had a used U-haul trailer, painted green and completely street-legal that could be attached to his car, which, to mention in passing, wasn't quite travel ready. The car's gas tank was kept together with plaster of Paris and the muffler was wired on with coat hangers. With these two moveable contraptions he toured the immediate country: Missouri, Kentucky, Ohio, Minnesota, Colorado (not through the mountains), Okielahoma, Nebraska, visiting art and craft shows that were glad to accept an artist of his caliber.

Whatever works he could afford to bring with him and sell almost paid the fare for these voyages, usually he'd get people interested in his works by presenting them his catalogue raisonné, and they would or would not make good on their promise to buy, later on. With this income, and the ten percent cut he got off finishing customers' work at the Gallery, he grossed enough to survive and rent a little house within the township of Winnsapeek, about a five mile trek from the workplace.

In his two-story farmhouse, he had a wife and three boys, none of whom were his by birth. The boys loved and respected him, tirelessly wanted to help him out at work, and Pablo raised them to do well in school. He also had a crazy dog named Olley. It would jump two feet into the air every time it saw someone it recognized.

His wife was a mystery.

His life was a daily grind. The beer of weekends and too much t.v. helped pass the time. Sure, there were excursions into the country, but this country was like western Texas, the hills wound with trees, deadly hot sticky nights in humidity and all night jazz stations playing, gravel in the announcer's voice. Live music and bars, one local establishment even had a velvet nude behind red curtains of the wall. But in this part of the country there were rarely ever killings. A few stabbings. Drunken fights leading to damage of broken chairs and tipped over beers, some broken glass.

Across Pablo's street in a little apartment built, or covered up thinly, to look like one really big house, the secretary lived. She was a secretary of a lawyer. She wore tight dresses, mostly always heels, which we all know murder the feet, died her hair a blond that just barely looked real. He watched her often, not really though, innocently, some would disagree, and he happened to notice her inordinately, maybe. Desire, he thought, is such a tricky thing.

As with poppies, follies. He was as loyal as a saint, his art was blushingly rife with religious, contemporary Judeo-Christian schlock, at least personalized in a way. Beaming face, with beard, never crucified. He had had loves in the past, namely with models, women and the occasional man of your or anyone else's dream.

In Osage, Missouri, the sales of a white plastic crucifix glued onto a cross section of native oak: $6.99. This piece of art has kept a devout family of five in business for thirty-four years. This same item at the Galley would be coated in wax, set on fire, a photo of it taken, a lithographic plate made out of the photo, and the resulting image, more so insignia, would be made in to an metal stamp trademark for a one-offed piece of heretical sculpture. This was the Gallery's modus operandi. Like what Stonehenge says about clocks, orreries, astrolabes, sextons.

The state of art cultivation in the middle west was so so. Pablo, though, was never discouraged. His bad-gone-worse affairs with his models helped him produce a multitude of nude pastels, which he sometimes had trouble showing in small local galleries. Inevitably, someone would complain about their lack of "wholesomeness" and a controversy would break out. This always helped him to sell a few, then find another place to display his work. The few he had hanging in the Gallery would bring in a some curious elder members of the Amish community, who would linger over them, for inordinate amounts of time, but the paintings never raised their dander.

Hence, Pablo's once hectic love life settled into a groove after he left his spawning place of Texas, where a nude picture of a woman would hardly bat an eyelash, when he came to the little corner of nowhere, his home of the recent six years.

His woman, into which he made a wife, was a local girl who had theatrical aspirations, and played in the cornstalk theaters around the area. It was rumored that she was a manic-depressive, really a thing hard to tell because she refused to come into the Gallery. Her reason: one artist was enough for her. What could be assumed about her was gained from hearsay coming from Pablo, and the evidence he brought with him. She cooked up a storm for him as evinced in his copious lunches he brought in and took an actual lunch hour to finish. Leg of lamb, stews of sausages, meat, and beans, whole chickens cooked in olive oil and potatoes and parsley, and he was more than willing to share his portions just for the asking.

He ate these meals with the same gusto that he worked on his and others' projects, as if it were the last, and a masterpiece at that. He would polish the food off with a gigantic plastic cup of sun tea, continuing the practice of brewing it from his southwestern days. Two spoonfuls of sugar.

One could surmise that his wife had one heck of a body, since one of his bronzes was modeled off of her. She sat in the corner of the exhibition room of the Gallery, seated upon a stone, knees bent and to the side, hands placed on thighs, breasts formed taught with golden worn nipples from the touching of curious spectators, keeping her head tilted and her auburn eyes on her man busy with work, life, and love.

But love is an illusion of familiarity and sex. Fleeting braids of life, like hair in the wind. Pablo found this out the hard, or some might say, the easy way. Before leaving for one of his tours of art and salesmanship around the immediate countryside, his wife dutifully helped him pack his heavy bronzes into his trailer. She made him meals to be eaten in the future: road food. Tupperware contraptions full of cold soup, stews, recently prepared meat and other such vittles. She made her children kiss him goodbye and wish him luck. She too wished him the best, and topped her farewell off with an afternoon of passion.

Afterwards, Pablo showered, trimmed his beard, looked over his reams of road and city maps, kicked his dog in the butt because it wouldn't stop following him, and took to the pavement.

He was gone for a week. He sold four pieces and did a little better than breaking even on the transactions. This was the goal and promise of the artistic cause: the ability to make enough to stay alive. He was ecstatic about his success and, after the craft show, enacted it by driving twenty miles over the speed limit, aided in part by the lightness granted by selling a few of his works.

Arriving at his home near ten p.m., he thought it strange that no lights were on, no kids running around the yard. As he approached the door, he saw a yellow post it note applied just above the handle. Behind the door, he could hear his dog whimpering in excitement.

She wasn't there. They weren't there. Most of the furniture was gone. The note read "goodbye honey, I love you."

Pablo thought it was a queer way to prove such a statement. Though he couldn't think. The house empty. Too quiet to do anything. He unhitched the trailer, left it in the front yard, and drove to the Gallery in tears. That night, he slept on the floor of the office. He slept in dust and dirt on a blanket reserved usually for Nora's old dog. He slept with his own dog next to him, its head near his head, where normally a pillow, instead of his rolled up shirt, would have been.

Women had left him before. When they did part, it was usually with the flourish of an argument featuring thrown objects derived from a kitchen or bar: glasses, plates, a water pitcher (full of lemonade), and in one instance, a dairy creamer. Pablo's reaction to his wife's disappearance was numbness and then the inevitable gnawing feeling that comes with the absence of a lover or anyone loved.

His nights became burdened by a vision. In four days, he found a studio apartment in the town square, across from a lawyer's office. The lawyer had a secretary who did not look small town. She had bleached blond hair, wore dresses that Pablo took great pleasure in describing as "slinky", and high heels of changing colors. It was her shoes that he began fixating on.

Talons, he started calling them. He started coming into work around nine a.m. Often his first sentence to anyone would be, "She was wearing them again. This morning." He began incorporating shoe-like curvatures and shapes into the clay models he was working on. He checked out books from the library on fashion, and footwear; he would sketch wild, beautifully and imaginatively crafted shoes on the wall near the telephone. He never referred to his wife, even when asked about it, shrugging his shoulders and shaking his head, mumbling something about the fact that he never not once treated her wrong.

Then he began to take photos. Using a telescopic lens through the lowered venetian blinds of his new place (he had no furniture and had taken to sleeping on the carpeting), he photographed, from the knee down, the secretary's legs. Scenarios presented themselves: bending to leave her car, legs crossed on the park bench while eating an apple at lunch time, once even she stopped on the sidewalk, lifted her foot backwards, removed her shoe to shake out a pebble, and this was captured on film by Pablo.

He had no bones about his latest artistic inspiration: he pasted these photos on the wall of the rubber room, to craft from them models in clay, at first, not of a high heeled shoe per say, but, abstractly of where the human foot intersected with the orifice of the shoe. It seemed he was interested with this point, this tangent of intersection, or better, insertion.

The men of the Gallery thought his new project to be a study in abstraction. It was only when he asked Nora and Alex, then Beth, for pairs of their old high heels, that everybody began to think this to be an unhealthy obsession. Pablo would say, out of the blue, at lunch, that Raymond's ham sandwich looked like bread filled with shoe leather. His conversations while working on plaster over-molds turned to questions such as why, in movies, do ecstatic lovers drink champagne out of a woman's shoe, never a man's. He imagined, out loud, what Cinderella's foot looked like in a glass slipper, and how a construction like that would feel, or even be usable. Why Mother Hubbard chose to live in one. And why was it that elves made them?

Lost for hours that churned themselves invisibly into days, then stacked themselves into months, Pablo worked, ate every now and then, and worked. He thought about this and this only: shoes. How

they were the things men and women put on when they were leaving.
How you take off your shoes when you get home, where it's sup-
posed to be safe, where you relax and finally, sleep. Why children are
ambivalent to them, how they constrict the wild electricity in their
little feet. How shoes disconnect one's connection to the earth, the
ground, like condoms that don't completely impede contact, but force
an unnatural barrier that wipes out the fur-like feeling of grass, the
grittiness of stones and gravel, the squish of mud and puddles. How
shoes transport us from one place to another efficiently as tools, car-
rying only the scuff marks of where we've been, the marks of what it
was like and the problems there encountered. Shoes stepping all over
themselves waiting in angst to be the pair used on any given day, anx-
ious to get out of the darkness of the closet. Shoes and the feet that
twist, deform, and shape them. Shoes tied in knots, and shoes, by the
door, tongues stuck out, laces undone.

The Dream of Mikey

A part-timer, jack of many trades and interests, Mikey did not know what he wanted out of life, or what to do in it, so he hung out and even managed to work a bit at the Gallery. He was naturally skillful, good at anything he tried—welding, polishing, making proto-type sculptures, inventing sculptures to be made, or at least drawings of them, and making love to unfamiliar women. According to his backroom stories, he was especially knowledgeable in the last category because he was continually in search for Ms. Right, or at least, her sister.

Symptomatic of many a mid-westerner born and bred in medium-sized cities, not having a particular accent and all too familiar with the forever stretching fields of corn and sometimes soybeans that led nowhere and contained nothing other than vast expanses of itself, he seemed to be seeking a horizon, a line of perspective, maybe a defini-tion of himself.

An early riser and smoker of morning cigarettes and addicted nail biter, he was the energy cell that got the Gallery going. The morning music thumping out of the lunch room stereo was his: funk, jazz, rap, or classical. He liked it all. When he worked, he liked to control the situation and job at hand; he was his own boss which meant there was an inevitable personality clash with Rex. After all, it was Rex's show, and he habitually called the shots even though he set unreasonable schedules that no one could meet and that demanded total commit-ment to the impossible.

Mikey and Rex carried out their psychic battle by leaving each other mean little post-it notes about the workplace. *If you're gonna do it like this, don't do it at all* by Rex would be met with a *If I don't do it, it won't get done, boss-man* by Mikey. There were times when Mikey's replies quoted philosophers or great men of literature; Rex would reply by intentionally illiterate responses misspelled on purpose. The best of these missives were culled by Raymond and left in the bathroom for the reading pleasure of all.

Thimk, next time, stoopid—R.

I thought, therefore I did—M.
Granpappa with his lame arm, could a done better—R.
Then get him to, pops—M.
Before finishing my pieces, ask!—R.
Because I did it better than you, don't be peeved, be happy—M.
Egads, it that a weld, or an iron caterpillar—R.
Neither, it's a pupa in molt—M.

In any normal workplace, these aesthetic exchanges would have lead to a firing before they could even be pronounced, in this case, writ, but this was the Gallery, and artists, up to a point, could be inspired and egos could be fueled by this kind of mental banter.

Because Mikey just didn't know what he wanted to do, petty arguments were a symptom. Partially, this is what led him to become engaged to his college sweetheart Karrie. Sometimes she would come in and wait for her man to finish work, and she'd bring a twelve-pack of beer for all. During these afterhours steam-blowing sessions, Mikey and Karrie would take little jabs at each other, in front of the others, revealing their unhappiness. Both worked marginal jobs—Karrie was a food preparatrice at a deli. Mikey worked at the Gallery. Both of them had no careers in sight for the future. They had children, in the form of two puppies, but they were just too young to be a couple, let alone a to-be-married one. When Mikey began sleeping at the Gallery, or in the back of it, in his car, the warning flag was unfurled.

It seemed that the artist's life lead to either infidelity or heartbreak, often both. When Karrie wasn't around, Mikey inevitably complained about his "set-up" to mainly uninterested ears. What could anyone tell him? There wasn't a success story in the ranks. Rex and Nora were always at each other, Raymond practically despised his girlfriend, Pablo's cut out on him, and Sam and Louise were never around enough to reveal the secrets of their bliss, which was, in fact, the true secret of their happiness.

During the long boring hours of drudge work, like endlessly sweeping up minute dust particles or re-arranging the tool shelves or collecting the tiny bits of pieces that didn't make it into art—from the floor, off the tables and desks, something Mikey loved to do, images of his possible wedding night drifted through his head.

Silver kegs of beer seeping flat beer, the band covering Hendrix tunes as inefficiently as they could, his buddies all gussied up in rented tuxes, his old flames looking better than they ever did when they were with him, especially the tall blonde who'd been in a motorcycle accident and had a scar running up her thigh, the dance floor of the non-denominational chapel barely occupied. A cafeteria fold-out table loaded with presents in beautiful wrappings that he'd later let his dogs in a fury open, his mother drunk on wine, attempting to sing the songs from her own wedding, the band reluctantly switching to Blue Moon, and her dancing with anyone who would dare. Somehow these visions didn't leave him sad, only wishing that they weren't his.

To say he wasn't happy was to miss the point altogether. He, like the others, wanted something better. He was selling some of his bronzes, especially the one of an ear of corn painted real colors and his giant iron cowboy boot. He even established a formula that took in all the costs, work time, even shipping fees, to gain a moderate profit. But days beginning with the thought of making ten or so belt buckles, out of bronze, that simply consisted of the words Belt Buckle put a damper on the crisp sunny mornings. Maybe he wanted to travel. Maybe he wanted to leave.

And he would, as often as possible. Usually, minutes of get away time. A walk to the gas station to pick up a pack of smokes and some candy bars. After putting in hours of reluctant work, he'd take one of his dogs out to the riverside park, watch the topographies of sinkhole and river form, then spin away, and he'd wonder what the woods looked like just beyond the levee on the other side. He'd roam the back alleys of town, where the Amish parked their horse and buggies, and he'd whistle and chirp to get their attention, then look for decent cardboard boxes from behind the thrift and hardware stores, for shipping his works to such distant places as Toronto, Okaloosa, Peoria, Albuquerque.

Other places is what Mikey often thought about. It is what lead him to buy a motorcycle. After the daily grind, he'd ride it along the highways that led from town to town, never actually going anywhere but around. With walkman earphones set snugly in his ears, and a helmet on his head, he could be elsewhere, almost with a feeling of flight, alone in the night air and wind listening to jazz turned up real loud. It was a mock escape from everything: his life, work, the country. To see lights of a town on the distant horizon, and to achieve them, downshifting past the police car in repose on the outskirts of the city, to cruise in third gear through the empty streets lit up by a local salon's beer sign and streetlights flickering through the wings of a million hungry moths. To accelerate outside of town, shifting, pushing the engine to its limits, entering a freeway, and opening up the bike to full speed, grinning, and facing the almost limitless possibility of highway 80—endpoints of San Francisco or New York—nothing stopping him but his own rationality.

One day he would just ride and keep riding. But not yet. Tonight, like most other nights, he'd go home, to his dogs and his woman, have dinner, watch a little t.v. until he became bored, and fall into another restless sleep knowing there was another day of hard work ahead of him, and that he was surrounded by fields and fields of fields, and that life was that way, but it didn't have to be, and he could change it if he wanted to, by leaving, by finding a different job, by having an affair, by drinking more, by whatever he wanted. The crux.

Knowing what to want was the hardest part. Karrie and Mikey would take trips to the big city, St. Louis, Minneapolis, or Chicago, to find the things that life in their corner of the woods lacked. Books, art museums, good restaurants, could from time to time provide the spark of excitement that once led them into the proposition of love. After a while, these places became the same old places, and they stopped going to them mostly because they tired of the long drives to them, always the same route, always the same familiar scenery.

Which, quite naturally, as all of nature is the antithesis of civilization, led Mikey to search for new landscapes within the limits of his territory. Landscapes of a highly localized and feminine disposition. Unable to find inspiration within his life, he began messing around.

He had for sometime been fascinated with the conceit of adultery, if there exists a person who is not, and started to test the clichés he'd learned from movies on women at nearby pubs.

Much to his surprise, they worked. Asking what sign a fellow drinker was, with a few initial laughs, proved to be a time tested true lead into a person's psyche. The third Scorpion he met in one evening garnered him a ride home, late, late at night, and a goodbye kiss and understood promise for a less crowded rendezvous. Her name was Monica and she was trouble.

Trouble came in the guise of abruptly disconnected phone calls. Mikey became forgetful of things, like where he put his keys and sunglasses; he'd drop sculptures he had just finished. At work, he started to blink uncontrollably, and stutter when he spoke to customers. Karrie began to pick up on these signals and the guys at work, being artists and never too far from the inspiration that only emotion could bring, knew something in Mikey's world had begun to become unhinged.

Especially since his bouts with Rex had almost completely subsided. This ongoing theater of dislike was one of the favorite vaudevilles of the Gallery. Without the tension between the two stubborn men, a dynamic was missing. Nora no longer had Rex's anger to console. Pablo didn't have a cohort in criticism of the boss. Alex couldn't act as mediator. Raymond sat and ate his lunches silently, trying to figure out what type of cloud was obscuring the co-op's weather. Then Monica started showing up at the Gallery.

Sam, who happened to be around only at the most crucial moments, announced her first arrival, from behind haze of blue generic cigarette smoke—*she's here Mikey boy, and dressed in nines.* And she was: heels, tight black pants, and a sweater that was more of a second skin than an article of clothing. When she arrived, Mikey dropped the ball-peen hammer in his fist, ripped the goggles off his face, and with a dirty handkerchief, wiped sweat and dust from his face. He ran into the bathroom to presumably fix his wild tuft of three o'clock work hair.

When he came out, Monica was chatting with the Raymond and Pablo in the office. *There you are*, she said when he entered the room, knocking over the cup of pencils on the desk. He invited her to the pub down the street for a beer and game of pool.

Mikey didn't come back to work that day.

Karrie called twice.

There is a type of psychic radar that infidelity, or the thought of it, breeds. When Karrie came into the Gallery at five thirty, the boys told her that Mikey was out with a client. Nora said nothing. Karrie didn't have to inquire about the gender of the foresaid client. It was understood. It's all in the eyes.

At the bar, Mikey and Monica small talked. Really mostly they didn't say much. Mikey watched her as she bent over the pool table, hands tightly holding the cue, one eye closed, one squinting when she made a shot. To him, she looked like an elf with dark hair. Angled eyes that looked maybe even Egyptian with the aid of carefully applied mascara. A perfectly proportionate pug nose, the tip of which moved when she smiled broadly. Long dark hair the color of fresh licorice.

She walked around the pool table, to make a shot, and bent her long body nearly an inch from Mikey's face. The thought that this couldn't be happening didn't occur to him. When she pulled her stick back, it hit his beer glass, which was on a wet napkin. The glass stayed position on its edge, tilted, holding half a beer. Mikey saw this as a divine sign.

So did most of the bar's patrons. They looked, laughed, pointed, then began to applaud. Monica smiled in astonishment before turning around and seeing what she had performed. She curtsied, took her shot, and sunk it.

To Mikey, this miracle was a message. And it read: *Caution Ahead.* Before he had the time to fully realize the situation, the time of late evening it was, his relative drunkenness, he was in the passenger seat and Monica was lighting a cigarette for him, in her mouth, and they were driving to her place.

When they got there, they were greeted by her auburn cat, Tether. Mikey entered, taking off his coat and apologizing for his grimy work clothes. Monica offered him a glass of wine, disappeared into the kitchen, from which immediately he heard the radio, the jazz station he always listened to. She came out with a bottle and two glasses and a lit candle.

This was something new. The taste of her lipstick. The contours of her body felt through tight jeans. Though she wore no perfume, her hair carried the scent of fresh picked flowers, or a newly used bar of soap. He tasted the taste of the gum she was chewing and didn't take out of her mouth. He measured her weight as it pressed down onto his own body, which he couldn't feel anymore. The buttons of her shirt were round and liquid smooth like seashells. She breathed his name, and something else that he didn't want to hear, then she bit his ear. It seemed as if her breasts were moving of their own volition. When he closed his eyes he saw Karrie's face, he saw his dogs running away from him in a big grassy field, he saw his mother scolding him for breaking a window with a baseball. When he closed his eyes, he saw the lights of some distant city slowing turning off, like stars dying. Mikey was going somewhere he had never been before, a new place, a location of no known address, somewhere where it might be possible to return from.

The Other Dream of the Country

Abandoned buildings. The things they left behind. Picture frames and photo albums. Shoes kept in boxes. Carcasses of cars. Flags stuck into the ground, faded and waving no signal. Barns built too close to the river, flooded and covered in a thin paste of dried mud. Trees and the husks of former trees. Animals and people and implements that have become dust and earth and ground. A carton of National Geographics left in the mud. A painting, in oils, of what someone thought mountains looked like. A clock museum. The world's smallest cathedral with a bell in a belfry that visitor's can ring, signifying visitation. Pumpkins lined up in a row waiting to be shot at with a twelve gauge. Dog leash chewed to frays, kept. Lifetime supply of handkerchiefs. Wild roses growing in a ditch. Supports of a bridge that are no longer needed, except to fish off of. Not much litter. Tame buffalo. Red shot gun casings burying themselves. Men in baseball caps walking in a field. The dinner bell ringing. Stale beer running down the gutter, emptied from still open bars. Iron stars left on brick buildings. Alleys and the smell of grease. Limestone bluffs remaining after the mine went bankrupt. Resulting sinkholes. Deaf ears of corn. Candles burning in windows. Spittoons rusted by spit. Owls in the rafters. Seeing people you know everywhere you go. Butt steak. Voices of Southern Christians on the radio. Fish jumping for mosquitoes at dusk. Get togethers in abandoned barns. Prairie thistle. Shrill cry of a fox. Falling in love with your cousin, the first time. Horses waiting to be ridden. Seasons sneaking up on the calendar, disguising themselves as years. Mornings arriving with angry crows. Letters arriving from Czechoslovakia at Christmas. Catfish frying in a pan. Trains whining through the night, shaking the house. Clean public rest rooms. Warped pool tables missing one ball anyway. The kids coming down with a bad case of poison ivy, or is it oak. Tornadoes and their anxious warnings. Pillows stuffed with down. Bushes frozen into ice that break when the cat runs through. Dandelions as evidence of spring. Clouds so low you can almost touch them, maybe hit them with a rock. Broken streetlights never to be fixed. A present for the postman. Night appearing as cold. The bellybutton of the new born saved in an envelope. Too much apple sauce. Blankets made from old clothes. Grandmother's menthol cigarettes. Arbor Day celebrated. Sunflower head drying in the sun. A nip of schnapps to prevent a cold. False deer or rabbits as lawn ornaments. Tool sheds filled with plastic jugs of old oil. Another child to fill up room in the family home. Stuffed monkeys made from socks. Bad paintings of a nordic Christ tacked up in the garage. More and more grocery stores. Piggy banks and slingshots never falling out of favor. A baseball tucked into the glove, well-oiled and tied up with a shoe string. Birdseed in fifty pound sacks. The garden overflowing with tomatoes. The leaves of last autumn never leaving. Dog buried in the yard. Church filled with parishioners late Sunday afternoon mass. Mushroom growing in the basement. Lightning the color of neon. Rumors of ghosts in the schoolyard. Nuns driving station wagons. A body found in a cornfield. Riverboats with slow paddles. Skating the streets after an ice storm. The theory and practice of scarecrows. Barbed wire and fence post. Ice cream stores locally made and owned. Illegal fireworks on the third, fourth, fifth and even sixth of July. Dead ends, cricks, ponds, and crawdads. Dirty magazines hid under leaf piles, or stones. Wild dogs that live in the woods. Remakes of ancient radio shows. Money from other countries displayed as art. Shelves of basket and footballs. Salvation Army stores that smell of mold. Bingo nights and pancake breakfasts. Mushrooms growing in the cemetery at night. Votives on sale. Eagles moving down river perched on ice floats. Laminated obituary bookmarks. Copper tea kettles. Daylight savings time miscalculated. Milk in bottles topped with cream. Cornstalk theaters. Raccoons visiting the gazebo. Mounds in the shape of animals undiscovered under tree cover. Homemade pies cooked for the priest, pans returned washed. Love letters written but never sent. Leaves pressed in the dictionary. Christmas ornaments kept in boxes that smell of aged cheese. Lightning bugs making the night into a reachable outer space. Sacred candles lit to scare away the storm. Brown eggs and cooked pumpkin seeds at the farmer's market. Children ringing the doorbell to ask for a glass of water. Robin, head cocked, listening for worms.

Wild strawberries near the railroad tracks. Cufflinks, wallets, thimbles, tape measures. A lost moose spotted near the strip mine lake. Seasonal reports of UFOs. Bluffs and the mountains they bluff. Shoe horns and dressmakers' dummies. Corncobs denuded to be made into pipes. Fields of clover weighed down by morning dew. Empty remnants of a zoo, painted red and blue. Mother explaining that staring at the mirror would reveal the face of Satan. Left-over pie crust rolled into cinnamon cookies. Birches peeling like onions. Piano no one plays humming in the open window gust of wind. Fireplace crackling with ash. Fishing poles no longer used. Names carved into the fence. Apple blossoms falling like snow. Hieroglyphs of dried worms on the sidewalk. Geese in a V arrowing north. Acorns wearing berets. Kids at the lemonade stand, no customers. The making of taffy. Bananas frozen onto popsicle sticks covered with chocolate syrup. Worms kept in glass jars. Snowballs from last winter in the freezer. Gate to the cemetery left open.

autumnal

FROM HERE TO THERE

"You've got to breathe," I told her. "You've really got to breathe, afterwards. I don't care how good it is."

"Oh, you don't care?" she asked from behind the black veil of hair that concealed her face. I couldn't see her mouth moving.

"You know what I mean."

Marie had a tendency to give her all, to go all out. She was really wild when we were together. But afterwards, she would stop breathing and lie there as still as a sleeping body. I would have to nudge her or watch her back to see it rise and sink, to see if her lungs were tenuously pulling on a thread of air. She could be so still. Sometimes she wouldn't say a word for a half an hour. Sometimes it scared me.

We were at the Blufftop Motel somewhere in the arid zone of southeastern Colorado. Our bodies and minds were drained as we both rested quietly while staring at the red glare of a digital clock. There must have been a recent storm that knocked the power out. It's common knowledge around here that you wake to sunny skies, clouds roll in late afternoon, it rains fiercely, then clears up. The rain stops you for a minute from whatever you're doing to watch the sun light up the dust in the air and extinguish behind cloudbanks that look like another distant range. It's been so long since I've been West I had to spot the scud and smell the cold dirty rain to remember what it was like. Most days it worked like clockwork.

The transparent white curtains were split open and in between them we could see a creme-colored plateau, streaked in green stripes of some kind of vegetation, maybe sage or juniper. I doubt pine, at least not yet. We hadn't come far enough to see a forest. This city seemed to be surrounded by tableland that was fissured into a million canyons like hidden mazes leading somewhere way beyond our gaze. And in them, the bones of dinosaurs sequestered. We would never find them though. Maybe no one would. Anyhow, we were just passing through.

We were going to the ocean. What we were really doing, who knows? Perhaps eloping. Maybe leaving our lives behind in a city where we had decent jobs and happy lives but not enough ways to get out. Maybe just taking a few days of vacation in the dying weeks of summer knowing we would return to our old selves safe and locked behind the deadbolt of an apartment's door.

The day after, we rose early and crossed Utah and the wretched desert of Nevada. The sun shone blindingly the whole morning of driving and our car hummed over the pavement like a well-oiled fan. She drove for hours with her eyes fixed on the unending slit, sometimes jagged, line of the horizon, switching the radio dial around to find any kind of music. Anything. A lot of rockabilly, low-budget classical, and whiny, excitable men talking about the divine tricks of Jesus. How Our Lord walked much the very same landscape as these wastelands speaking of fecundity and the God in man. How he could make wine out of water and fish out of nothing but stones in baskets.

I was seeing the illusions of Palestine myself come to life in the vapors of heat above the highway. A sidewinder was really only a streak of orange desert sand brought to life by a gust of air. The mountains in the rearview weren't moving and the Santa Fe train line underlining them wasn't moving backwards. The wooden sign marking the playa couldn't have said "next exit 150 miles."

There were tens of different brands of gas stations and hastily erected warehouses. Sometimes a Calder of a refinery lit up with circus lights. I thought of ranch houses on the moon. Cattle trails were ground into the land like directions cut for the single engine airplanes flying above us. The few cactuses were in bloom with feathered hats of yellow and orange-like red.

"Pull over!" Marie yelled, waking me from my road dream. A rooster tail of dust enveloped the car. She ran out, leaving the door open, onto the scrub and piñon of wilderness. Flinging her leather purse along, at full-sprint, into the dying light of the desert, where the only cover was bush and rock streams of arroyos. Her glasses were sitting on the dashboard, fingerprints about the edges of the lenses.

Fourteen minutes passed before she was back. Her hair in switches and her cheeks blushed by the wind.

"What'd you do?"

142

"I had to pee. It's really beautiful out there. Everything's alive. Even the dirt. I think I saw a scorpion. There was something out there. I mean I saw something moving on the ground."

~

We guessed we were still in Nevada. Tumbleweeds and gray stone hills in rows like monuments to nothing. The gas stations petered out on the highway where only fence poles marked the highway's direction and served as civilization's minimalism. A mantle of cool air was descending. A naked hand on the windshield left a stain of condensation. I began, I believe, seeing cradles of fog here and there, ghosts of clouds for seconds under the brights. Seeing is believing.

Marie drove for the rest of the night. One arm on the door, the other changing the dial or adjusting the mirrors. I wondered: to see what? She found a station that was on the frequency of short wave, emitting only beeps of sound, static and eerie feedback "There," she said "that's it."

When I woke, we had come all the way to Sacramento. The plains rolled at the same speed as us and buckled into a crease of hills behind. After them, the ocean. Further west, Asia. She pointed to a jack-knifed trailer. Four cars had piled up behind it. There was an ambulance and the few cars of traffic were slowed down at the scene. A man lying on a stretcher, tied to it, with a reflection of red in his eyes similar to that of a wolf's I thought I saw once as a boy in the north woods. Two men were carrying him to the open doors. He could have been seeing angel wings. The Greek becoming visible in the blue writing on white background: PARAMEDIC.

We had miles to go before we would reach the Grapevine, then the unending patchwork of Los Angeles, if the city could be seen under the blanket of early morning fog to be replaced by the opaque grey of afternoon pollution. We had arranged a place to stay somewhere along the coastal highway. It was an abandoned shack on the beach that was formerly used as a summer house by Marie's sister who worked from time to time as a writer for television. She was now in between jobs and wanted the consolation of company. We would stay there and visit her in her new place in the hills. She warned us that we might become enchanted by the larger than life billboards on the road to her house and would never want to leave the glorified brand of reality that Southern California breeds. She referred to the region as "So Cal."

~

"You wanna drive now?" Marie yawned.

"Sure."

The suburbs began and never did they cease. There was so much visual stimuli that I could barely keep my eyes on the road. Road sign. Call box. Weeping willow. Little Saigon. Traffic light. Palm trees ruffling their feathers in the breeze. We had made it to the end of a continent. The odometer changed over. Warm air filtered through vents and smelled of pavement and ocean sand.

A sidewalk extended into the sea. On the concrete platform, the iron railing had rusted to a deep maroon. Blotches of deep blue paint remained like thumbprints of limpets. Wooden benches with mainly seagulls aligned on them. It smelled of the cheap seafood restaurants burdening the pier. The word crab in Chinese and an airbrushed watercolor of the bright orange spider on a poster fluttering on a false kiosk. Marie got out of the car. The ocean was just across its empty parking lot.

The Santa Monicas leaned into the water, green in the distance, a mist beginning around their base and the lip of the ocean. The arcade was lit up. There were the musical chords of a carnival.

The first thing Marie said was "Oh shit."

"Look, it's not that bad. There's seagulls, a mist coming in, look at that, down there, those models. It looks like they're doing a fashion shoot!"

There were women dressed to kill behind lights and some men in leather. One had a camera. Another was telling the women where to stand.

"My pants. They're ruined."

I looked over the top of the car. Marie had a dark halo around her lap. What she called her monthly curse had followed her. I remembered the cactuses in bloom.

"So what," I said. "Put a long shirt on. We're here."

We walked along the pier breathing it all in. At a tall, wooden building that had the word "Sinbad's" painted on it, we stopped. It was abandoned but once must have been an arcade or a bar. Its gabled roof with warped planks peeling apart from one another seemed really western even if it wasn't. Truth was the only thing that wasn't a commodity in this town, maybe even this era.

The continent lay behind us. If there is such a place, or feeling, or state of something called happiness, we had found its momentary location. But like a hungry seagull, it took off on the next ocean breeze.

Marie, with her eyes scanning the distance and the ends of her hair feeling for the salt in the air, said, "Well, we made it. We really made it."

"Where's that?" I asked.

"From there to here," she whispered. We breathed in the iodine of coastal air.

THE BLUE SKY

Music, as thick as the smell of grease, was floating in the slight breeze behind El Cielito Lindo. It was the Mexican-American equivalent of happy hour at the restaurant and the margaritas had begun to flow. The men in the alley were smoking swisher sweet cigars and talking loudly about whatever—cars, the weather, women, the rope burns on their hands. Narcisco and Lydia had just been married and the reception had finally begun to get loud. The accordion players, there were three of them, were crooning a song of love gone awry. No mater how appropriate it was or not, the people seemed to enjoy it, slowly crowding the dance floor in pairs. They stopped their two-steps occasionally to pin dollar bills on the bride's wedding veil and to sing along in Spanish to the verses they recognized.

I was taking a break from it all. I found a swimming pool closed for the day in the Cordoba apartments behind the restaurant. Surrounded by a concrete patio that had plenty of lawn chairs, the waters of the pool were calm and I propped my feet up and leaned back to sip my beer. If only I had some salt for it. The gate surrounding it was locked, but there were a couple of bars of the fence that were removed. Just enough for a gringo to squeeze through. Yolanda couldn't bother me out here. Not unless she jumped the iron fence. It was nearing dusk and the heat, 108 degrees today, was beginning to diminish. The breeze helped as it moved through the fronds of the palm trees. Finally a quiet moment of the day. Pigeons in the trees cooed at my presence that was becoming mere shadow.

It was true, what the men were saying. I had known Lydia. After a month of work picking spinach in her brother-in-law's fields, she decided to invite me to dinner in her trailer on her father's ranch. She was renown for her skill in making tamales, and she would make hundreds of them at a time in a large tin bucket on the stove to feed the laborers at lunch time. But the dinner was a private affair, which was something I didn't realize until I showed up, still in my work clothes. I thought that others were coming, but when no one else showed, I sat down, relaxed and ate like a horse, hardly saying a word or even looking at her.

Afterwards, when she left the table to put a Flaco Jimenez disc on the victrola, I knew I was in trouble. She began to tell me that she had never had a gringo over for dinner. I told her that I was only half American. My father was a migrant worker and my mother was a Baptist and nurse in the Salvation Army. My mother with the beautiful strawberry hair. Then she asked if all of my hair was so blonde, as light as my mother's. Her Spanish was ambiguous. I can still remember the words to the song:

> *My Texas girl is so beautiful*
> *There is no one else like her*
> *Her kisses give me life*
> *Her gaze brings me to tears*
> *She is my joy*
> *She is my desire*
> *She consoles my heart*
> *She has black eyelashes*
> *And her mouth is like a ruby.*

From a breeze that blew through the alley of the restaurant, I could hear a similar melody charging the languid air.

I could also hear Yolanda calling my name. She wasn't exactly my girlfriend, more like the type of woman who looks out for men who she finds attractive, or just as lonely as herself. She too, with her long auburn hair and gray eyes, was of mixed blood and could understand my feelings. Like when I attempted to dance with the bride and her family asked me not to. I guess I understood their desire. But it was in the way they put it: so as not to spoil the festivities. So I'm sitting this one, and every one after, out. Yolanda is nice but she doesn't know everything about my past. And she'll never think to look for me out here. It's getting too dark.

Not that it matters at this point, but I have no grievances with Narcisco. We first became acquainted when we were working beets together in Montana. The first thing he ever said to me was, "You have some country here." He pointed to a place off in the distance where the mountains intersected a horizon of prairie. I laughed and told him that it was as much my country as it was his. Just because I held dual citizenship at one point of my life didn't mean that I had any control over my future in the vast fields of America. He didn't understand this and treated me like one of his friends. We shared a bottle of Tequila that night and told each other homesick stories. This was way before my encounter with his future wife. He had many stories of the road to tell, stories of hardship and drunkenness. Since it was my first tour of labor in the North, I didn't have much to counter with. So I told him the story of his name. I remembered the myth from my school days as a child growing up in Douglas, Arizona.

He especially enjoyed the part of Narcissus gazing at himself in the water only to become a flower. He told me that he too liked flowers and that his favorite one was the rose of jericho. It would be many years until I had found one while hiking through the desert. I had never encountered such a lovely and intricate plant before. I should have picked it from the hard soil.

The only funny thing about this whole affair was the plain fact that Narcisco wanted to get married. Lydia wasn't even pregnant, or at least she didn't know it yet. I can't quite understand where his urge to get married came from. Especially with people like us, who will never have the stability of a decent job. We are the kind who will always have to be on the road doing the same back breaking work with only the location, from one month to the other, changing. My favorite place is California, with its long, strange hills and its grape growing valleys. How the mornings are mist-filled and cool and the days not too humid.

It probably has to do with age. You get to be a certain number that was figured out at birth, maybe it has to do the number of hairs on a baby's head or with the whorls in one's fingerprints. For some, it's a low number: eighteen or twenty-two. Once a man achieves that marking in years, he must take a bride and create another. There really can be no choice in the matter. How else could one explain it with a man like Narcisco whose reputation with, first, the bottle, and then, women, is so legendary. Of course, he didn't seem to have such luck when he was on the road with the rest of us, but he does know girls in all the cities we work. He just doesn't seem the marrying type. He's twenty-nine years old.

Luckily, I'm still young. Yolanda thinks I'm a child. When I rejected her the first time, in the back of Ramiro's truck at the drive in, she asked me if I was a man yet. I told her about the many women of my past: the girl in Idaho, the ones in Arizona, and the girl I met in Texas who wanted me to move in with her. She was a secretary and easily made enough money for the two of us to live well. Yolanda doesn't believe me though, and cites my willingness to return to these shanty towns of the border lands as proof at my failure as a lover or even, a man. I will let her believe that because she will never know the truth. She will never know who I really am.

The truth is I am still a kid. I wouldn't be wise for me to take a bride at the age of twenty-four. If I did, then I would never get out of this life, not that I want to at the moment. Working the fields is all right for now and I make a good wage as long as I spend it south of the border. Someday, if I want, I will live somewhere better, like San Diego, and have a car and a house and a dog. There's no need to rush. It really is a big world. Even bigger than the invisible borders I have crossed.

From this distance, I see the men in the alley setting the rose-covered trellis on fire. It is consumed in flames in what seems like seconds. It illuminates the graffiti on the walls. There's an awful attempt at a mural of Zapata– ammo belts slung over his shoulders, although it looks like he's wearing a Stetson. I wonder what he thinks of his children tonight?

I can hear them talking about going down to the river to continue the party and start a real bonfire, like they usually do on the weekends. My friends like it down there on the sand bar even though the river is mostly a dry bed. They'll probably shoot at the owls that roost on the abandoned railroad bridge. I'll go with them to watch the moving stars of big American jets pass overhead and sit in the warm sands with my boots off.

I'm sure Yolanda will come too and ask me to teach her about the dark blue sky. I still remember a few of the constellations. It's really too bad that this gate surrounding the pool is locked. The water is so still and glows from a light underneath. I bet the men would love a midnight swim, even with the stupid body of a drowned bat floating in the pool. Poor animal, it was probably just thirsty and didn't know what it was getting into.

It is getting late, I can hear a guitar strumming and my name in the wind. It must be Yolanda who is looking for me. Yes, it is probably Yolanda who is looking for me, for a ride to the riverbed. It is Yolanda who is calling me and singing the words to a song that she doesn't even know.

ADVICE

"Make me your myrrour"
—George Gascoigne, 1575

They say it will take some getting used to. The change of scenery. From hills that barely sloped (a trick of distance) to these mountains lined with spears of trees. They say it is the weather that will convince me. They ask me if I like clouds. I assure them that I do like clouds.

They say that when it snows, the city changes dramatically. They say the snow whitens everything for the day, then disappears in the afternoon sun. The seasons here seem to be intermingled: mornings in winter, afternoons in fall, and summer sunsets all year round. They say the effect is of time extended; days last weeks, weeks last months, years last eternities.

They say the people are friendly. That they'll do anything for you, if only asked. They say they're congenial and are given to having sociables and parties, but rarely live outside their own dwellings. You seem to never see them in their yards, pruning trees or mowing the lawn. Other people do that for them. In the countryside, some keep hex signs painted on their barns that their ancestors believed in. They bring good luck and keep misfortune hungrily concealed in the woods.

They say things like "in good time" and "resources permitting" and "if there's a will there's a way" and "only time will tell". They seem to mean well. They say "it's always been this way" and "worrying will only wrinkle your brow." They nod their heads confidently and look away or scratch at a cuticle.

They are quick to open an old photo album and begin to unravel their stories. Here's what the town looked like before the highway: see the cottonwoods lining both sides of the river. Here's the old Unitarian church. A steeplejack came once a month. Here's old Indian's Point where there still lie the bones of saguaros, skeletons of their teepees. This building was a whorehouse; now its a restaurant and bar. Here's Mrs. Holden's home, a spinster who held tea parties; now it's a museum. Here's the railroad men's house, barracks really; now it's a travel agency. It all seems to make sense.

They say the wilderness surrounding contains priceless artifacts of both indigenous peoples and colonists. They say the rattlesnakes own them now. They say you're welcome to reclaim them anytime. They say: wear boots.

They say it's all how you choose to see it. They say it's in the finding of one's bearings. They say don't count your marbles. They say it's in the music of the spheres. Seems it always has something to do with little balls.

They say it could be worse. They say they saw kids in the alleys of a foreign country they visited. They say they spat into jars. When the jars were full, they say, and the night air chilled them, the kids would drink it to stay alive. They didn't say what they ate. They say the boxes behind the groceries were always empty.

They say blank walls invite the possibility of pictures.

They say traffic makes sense. They say that people like to talk to one another in crowds, on the bus, while shopping, whenever. They say this is bred into their kind: good manners and thoughtful minds. They say you could fall in love going to the bakery for a loaf of day old bread.

They say it has to do with the humidity. They say the air curls the covers of books open. They say it's great for your hair. Even though it might be hard to breath from time to time. They say it's like running uphill underwater.

They say you don't need watches here. They say that clocks are put on every wall of every building. They say there are three bell towers downtown. Ringing precisely every hour, half hour. They say it always sounds like Christmas.

They say that hardly anyone wears sunglasses. They say it's rude. When I passed a couple at a sidewalk café talking with their glasses, and hats, on, they said: "Look at the corpses chatting."

They say it's what you put into it, not what you get out. They say it's a matter of time. Not the time of the matter. They say that they enjoy planting tulip bulbs in the cool mid-evening air. They say they can see tulips growing into the larvae of butterflies below.

They say Wednesday, Thursday, Friday, it doesn't really register. People do what they do whenever. They say it's true, the shops have to eventually close. But they say that most of the time they can do without what's in them. It just takes ingenuity, a hammer, and some string.

They say remember the seven hills of Rome.

They say they know of all the best restaurants and will take you there. They say they'll order the wine, all you must do is drink it. They say its been years since they've seen salad forks. They say the waitresses are beautiful, that you can't see their real faces beneath the make up. They say have some more wine, the prices are reasonable.

They say blood is thicker than water. Oil heavier than vinegar. Smoke more white than milk. Scissors more lethal than paper. Rocks that fit in the palm of your fist.

They say it takes all kinds. They say that through the windows, if it's an old house, the outside seems bleary, wavy. They say you will mistake leaves moving on a branch for birds. They say milkmen still deliver bottles to the backdoor. They say the cream on top is the sweetest if warm. They say broken glass is everywhere in the streets. They say they recycle nothing here.

They say they have never been to Tegucigalpa. But they have heard stories.

They say it's not who but what you know. They say they have friends who have been struck by lightning. They say they have lived to find that they are better people for it. They remember more, they have premonitions, they never suffer from the chills. They say they always know, hours before, of the oncoming storm.

They say that they have had operations. Small ones. Tonsils removed or a tattoo erased. They say that the wisdom teeth are really a burden and that the knowledge they contain soon leads to decay. They say that the teeth of the natives are worn smooth by eating so much grit and sand. They remind you that teeth once made beautiful jewelry.

They recommend doctors, insurance agents, interior decorators, and veterinarians. They say that the parrots in the pet stores all come from Mexico. They say beware of the centipedes sometimes heard scurrying through the walls. They say they breed like mice.

They say there is a local crime scene. They say they produce their own pornography, make imitation drugs, run a stolen car racket. They say always lock your doors and windows. They say the afternoon is more dangerous than night.

They say the squirrels act differently here. They say that they'll sneak into your cupboards and find the almonds you were saving for baking. They say they'll bury them in a thousand different places in the yard or park nearby. They say, come winter, they won't forget the location of even one.

They say there is no way of getting around it. The grocery stores are crowded on weekends, the bookstores empty. They say that the freeways are easy to drive because everyone usually stays in one or the other lane. They say the drivers are courteous and smile at you while stopped at red lights.

They say if you stay you'll become accustomed. They say the city has its own rhythm and cycles. They say you must get used to the late mail, the erratic hours of the stores. They say once your schedule is melded into the daily routine, everything makes sense. They say the clocks run faster in the fall than the summer. When they insist on this, you are not sure if they want you to stay and see.

They say not to mention the fifth season, what they call winter's spring. They say warm air from the Gulf envelops the area and the grass grows green again. They say it even fools the porcupines who leave the hills in search for food. They say they usually end up dead in the gutters, like so many discarded pincushions.

They say its a trick of distance. That the city isn't as big as it seems. But you can find anything here you want. Though nothing that you were looking for.

They say that there's one in every crowd. They say this place is conducive to loners, drifters. Just check out the bus station. There's people sleeping on park benches with only bundles of necessity: sleeping bags, styrofoam cups, burnt pages of magazines stuffed into plastic bags. They say they're trying to remedy this. There are ordinances, they say. There are always ways to tie up the loose ends.

They say on clear nights you can see Saturn but not its rings.

They say that the inverse is always true. For every new arrival there is a departure. They say when the day ends the night begins. And darkness is conducive to thought. When the beautiful scenery disappears, its spell recreated in the millions of quaint brick houses.

Each with its potted plants and Christmas lights so carefully strung. They say holidays here are unequaled. That the citizens are a festive bunch. That the fireplace is an altar of ceremony. They say sagewood burns most brightly when culled from the deserts beyond. They say that oak only quells the flame.

They say travel is inevitable. Although there isn't anywhere to go. They say the lake is impenetrable and winter casts a spell on the surrounding plains. They say the fun is in the journey to nowhere and the seat of this destination is your home.

They say they are proud of the clean boulevards. They take serious pride in manicuring their gardens and yards and parks. They say kudzu wouldn't have a chance here. They say dandelions are poisonous.

They offer you tips. They suggest getting to know the mailman, the local pastor if you're so inclined. They have parties and dim the lights. They say we all are a family unto ourselves.

They show you pictures of their pasts. Vacation photos of places you will never go. They say it's always so good to be back. They say "into the fray" and "shoulder to the grindstone". They would lead you to believe in the eternal return. But they know you can never leave.

They say it's a perspective rarely seen. They say there are no enemies, but there are gates.

They ask you what you think so far. What you like and dislike. They seem to think you can only repeat what they already know. That reason will find its rhyme, that maps will eventually reveal directions, that monkeys here never escape from the zoo. They say they are most happy when there is nothing to do. They say you will find this to be true. They agree to agree and so you do.

LAKE SHORE DRIVE

Her name is Marta Anitolova and I love her. These are the facts. The mere facts. I won't be so crude as to call them statistics. Five foot nine and one half inches tall. 123 pounds. She likes books, photography, music, t.v., and cooking. In her own words: "without children, without a past, congenial, blond hair, eyes blue, hide white."

These are the details she chose to advertise. As if her picture were not good enough, she had to throw in the last bit. She said that it got her many, many letters, mostly from older men. Yes, mainly perverts and not exactly who she hoped would write. She wrote that she was looking for a true connoisseur of all earthly things: a poet, you see. This is what she said.

Her name is Marta Anitolova and I love her. I am the one who wrote her the letter. Four and a half months ago. I am the one who sent my picture. I put this thing into motion and now I can't stop it. I don't know if I want to stop it. We are going to get married. We are going to get married again and again.

It was so simple. On Saturdays, at the post office, if it's open and the few clerks inside aren't too busy mailing their own letters with their hands moving furtively under the counters, it's possible, for a second, to get one's attention: the mailman who isn't pulling delivering duty. Ask him where the WANTED posters are. He'll point over the glass case opposite side of the vending machines and stamp administering devices in the shapes of stainless steel safes. Right to the glass case of posters. Criminals on the make for things mundanely illegal. Their faces hardly distinguishable from the bad photocopies and the plain ugliness of one another. Look in the garbage can right next to this.

You see, proximity never lies. In the big plastic container there it was tossed. Inert. Its pages barely paged through. I picked it up. A green catalogue. It could have been a stamp collecting book. But it wasn't, it really wasn't. Who knew that it was possible to order women from a book. Mail order brides. Some even were women in among all of those too, too young girls. And all I wanted to do is to see if there were any interesting miscreants passing through town. I wasn't including myself.

There are girls from Malaysia. There are girls from Hong Kong. There are girls from Sweden. There are girls from Argentina. The Philippines and Peru. Girls from Tokyo and Gdansk. The are girls from everywhere, of any hair color, preferably blonde or brown it seems. Some attempts at the sultry redhead type. They like everything a general reader could like: movies, sports, fine dining, and would give their addresses for a small, really insubstantial fee. All the interested party had to do is agree to pay for her address. You would correspond. Trade pictures. Write about your dreams a little. Then they'd arrive for free, if they could make the air fare. In your hometown. Or the nearest Chicago.

Where am I in the third world of one of these cafés near the train station that goes to the airport? The shadows of buildings are weighing heavily on the streets. People walk by the window holding the two halves of their coats tightly together as if concealing a freshly cut wound open against the cold.

I don't smoke but am smoking to fire up the waking of the day. This is real cheap inspiration. The coffee is good. The coffee is always good here. The food, well. The view of the traffic is enthralling. The sides of buildings are still frozen blue. It's going to be morning for a while. I don't have to leave the warmth of this place. Clinking of plates and a murmur of rumor based on only what the magazines, latest best sellers, and Sun-Times are saying. Nothing, or the time it occurs in, is completely futile. The hands are winding on the dimly lit face of the clock. Salt shaker of cinnamon for my one cup of cappuccino. Bought my drink with coins found in my car seat.

~

Her name in Marta Anitolova and she loves me. If I try I can visualize what she is doing at this moment. She has taken a cab to the airport of her city that is located out in the fields of wheat that surround it and, towards their farthest ends, crinkle into the folds of foothills. There is a chain of high, white peaks that underline the clouds south of the city. These monoliths separate northern Europe from the rest. They run east to west in the shape of a question mark. She no longer visits their solitude, not since she was a child and learned to ski in a matter of hours. She skied so well that she was passing her father on the slopes as a streak of blue. A cap with a ball she wore on her head.

The cab she rides in is an old American car that smells of years and years of stuffed ashtrays. It's brand name is Imperial but there is nothing royal about it except for the space it allows. She can easily fit in its backseat with her two suitcases resting on either side. Everything else she burned in the felled tree pit of her family farm. She has distilled her life down to the clothes that she is known to wear. She thinks that she too will dispose of these luxuries as soon as she can buy western jeans and blouses and sweaters for a reasonable price. She cannot wait to see herself in the mirrors of this country.

When she arrives at the airport, her driver will offer her, first, assistance, then, a cigarette. She will decline both and pay him for the fare and tip him magnanimously. He will be graciously surprised as he slides back his sailor's cap and clenches a Gauloise between his stained teeth. She will not look back through the wide, high glass windows of the airport out onto the trash fouled streets that lead to nondescript buildings of grey steel and white concrete. Buildings that look like mail. Streets that circle nowhere.

She will struggle with her bags oblivious to the men dressed in suits, (some even of Italian make), who acknowledge the anomaly of her existence there. Especially in such a dress and with bare legs, feet fitting snugly into her black high heels as she walks by the news-stand where there are displayed magazines and newspapers and maps. They all are so different yet attempt to sell one thing. The same thing.

There is one newspaper, a thin thing really, that is printed in English and consists of articles pulled from various British and American magazines. The ink of the letters is already fading after only days and the news itself barley clings to the yellowing pages. The events it pictures in black powder and smudges is days old. Not even news at all, but she buys one anyway to practice her reading skills. On the landing airplane she will mouth these foreign words silently to herself as she rises from her seat to continue the alexandrine beat of her un-interrupted progress across the tiled floor. Tee-tock tee-tock tee-tock tee-tock tee-tock-tee-tock–

~

The smell of badly cooked hamburgers is in the air. With me is my bag. I keep an attaché full of things that I can't ever seem to throw away. This includes: lint and tobacco leaves, Swiss army knife (with magnifier), a pencil severely bitten, bent paper clips partially unwound, a calculator stolen from a previous job, a harmonica body, keys to I don't know where, half of a dollar bill (muddy), and other things stuck in the corners in the folds of the crevasses. Some might even consider it a purse. And, of course my files and my portable.

I carry stuff around like a fingernail carries dirt. Wonder if she'll think this about me or what she'll think about not having to get a job, to not really work and see what life is about. When she realizes that what I do is not even work; that the paintings I sell and trade, she can never know anything about. Like the Corot copy that only two people know of. How can I not tell her about the painting I found under the Degas. And not a word about the Munch. How will I be able to conceal such screams?

Perhaps the apartment will impress her, divided into two views of this big and distant city. The special effects of buildings at night, those showy temples lit up in halogen. The lake on the other side with its urban beach to no private ocean. Sketches of it in books I have but they aren't very detailed. Like the fog that settles at the lip of the shore some mornings all the way to Milwaukee.

Will she believe any of this?

In my pockets I have the directions. They're as plain as a pinkie toe. Flight number blah, blah, blah at whatever, whatever gate. She'll be standing there. No, I won't be holding a red carnation. I have her picture. I know what she looks like. I seem to know what she's like. I seem to know what she's about. And it's all about *the seems*.

She has seen me in a picture, too. I was much younger then, I had such wild hair. Everything was blurrier back when I was into photography. I did a lot of portraits of people I knew but I'm not sure if I know them now. Even their pictures have changed. Faces are better to remember than names. There's William with the gold tuft of hair, Madeline and Ellerby, Dade, Rhonda with the strawberry braids, Danielle whose name I think I've forgotten, Maxwell, Stephen, Cranes of the perfect beard, Lottie, others. The thing is I know they remember me. At least I'm a memory. At least I think I am.

Marta Anitolova will love me. She will carry a small present for me in her arms. It will be hand crafted wooden eggs or a pair of shoes from her country or it will be a phrase that she has been remembering over and over for the last hair-raising three hours. Something said if not in perfect English, then pronounced in the heart. *This is perhaps?*

There will, as there always will be, a run in her stocking that reaches from her knee to the creases of her heel. Her hair will be done. Her eyes as green as in the polaroid, chemicals still swirling around in them. Her skin as white as the bloodless bones in my hand clenching the keys to my car. Our car, our apartment, our body connecting in a first round of awkward, obligatory sex. We will sleep in each others arms or at least try. How we will cling to what we believe is each other.

She will see me as her savior, her agent of release, her spy of love. Or will I be just one of the many that she has known and if, if she is beautiful, a real beauty, will she use me to get into the country and dump me at the next available opportunity? The red tape flows much looser here than back there, the old country.

Maybe this place will be too much. The circus of our initial rendezvous: the airport. The vendors and all the different kinds of food they sell. The hotdogs with relish and zucchini spears, the lewd triangles of pizza, ice cream in all of its forms. None of it ethnic. None of it real. What we will eat tonight. In this city, the food is twice as hearty. I'm banking on pasta and its universality. There is always good wine. Even if it's only for our table.

Her name is Marta Anitolova and she is looking for me near the escalator, holding a green package and a fifth of vodka in a plastic bag. Her hair is in a bun that is streaked with strands of auburn. The high heels she wears are deep purple, not black. They match her makeup, barely brushed on. Her nose is pug. Her eyes are wide. Her dress is black. Her hands are free of rings, her nail polish clear and natural. Her teeth are small and perfect. She is smiling and walking towards me as if she knew where she were heading. She is blushing. She smiles again with tears this time welling up in the corners of her eyes. She takes my hand and squeezes it.

She says, "Hello. My name is Marta. Marta Anitolova."

THERAPY 5 CENTS

As I sit on a beige couch and look out my therapist's window I cannot help to be annoyed by the new age music she plays to get her patients in a mellow mood– like music for infants who have trouble falling asleep. The view is this: hills, the lumps that surround the East Bay, green because it's spring and clumped with oak trees and other secret spots for deer to hide. The occasional rows of boulders that haven't moved in ages. What am I doing here? Oh, that's right, I'm insane. Or, do I merely have issues? I mean, we all have issues. Don't we?

I guess I could easily fall asleep in here: the lulling, psychotropic music does sort of grow on one, the heat that is much too high, and she is here to finally keep me safe, at least for one hour. See, to BE here means I'm not crazy and she tells me so and I have to believe her, blue irises behind cat's eye glasses. It's all that an insane person needs, for a moment. Like a drug that really works.

She dresses in Oriental-esque clothes: a Chinese chemise that has big round buttons on top that she fidgets with. She is a beautiful woman, in her late fifties. Brown hair, a certain lack of sun damage that makes her look forty something. And she'll listen to me and my nightmares and fantasies. I'm fully aware that this is friendship prostitution and she knows it to. That's what makes it something less than creepy. What is this therapeutic moment: two people connecting for 59 minutes, I guess. Me hiding my desire; she holding back yawns. It's a game we play that no one ever really wins.

I'm here because I can't take it anymore. The economy, the wars, the interpersonal relationships we make that pan out into less than gratifying sex or e-mails that are full of such woe and self-pity they burn the eyes. Because she is a therapist who reads for pleasure and I'm a patient with literary aspirations we synch on some level. We are in some sense one and the same. She listens to my stories, reads popular lit like "More Tales of the City", I read and write tales of modern urban angst, and we both think we know something about the world out there, where there are constantly sirens and the sounds of people peopling the silence. We know that both of what we do is supposed to actually make a difference but it doesn't, in the larger scheme of things. Perhaps on some level of a Dante-esque hell what we do matters, but in a culture of instant gratification, a sin we can't stop sinning, how can we really change anything? Let's face it: no one out there can focus more than three minutes. It's the pop song mentality syndrome.

What we'll talk about today is always the special on the menu of possibility. I'd be lying if I were to say I'm not here more to pick her brain than resolve anything in mine. For her to be normal or seem normal with all the terrible stories she must hear, the whining and complaints, the verifiable psychoses, and how each time we both trust her ability to dress beautifully, I really do not know how she copes. Trips to a time share in Cabo; a wedding in Copenhagen. When I think of those vignettes, I do not fully get how they could satisfy her inquisitive mind.

I feel like such a whore.

I live in a vast toilet bowl, or, at least, on its fringes. It's called the Bay of San Francisco and people desperately cling to its seat in their horrible 50s, 60s and 70s style houses (tract) in a belief that this is the promised land. Don't get me wrong: it's a beautiful toilet bowl, exquisite mountains and the mirror of the bay. There should be a calendar of beautiful toilet bowls. Liberace must have had a great one or twelve. But this promised land comes with a price that is anywhere from two to ten times the price of living anywhere else, except New York City, in the meaningless puzzle that is America. The truly rich or truly rich wanna-bes live in San Fran herself and on the hills that surround. Think of the Hollywood hills minus the film industry and in its place, the bizness of Hi-Tech anything, and the cut-throat business of money. This is where all the world's, or much of its, technological crap is produced, marketed, and sold to the sheeple. Look how far technology has advanced us: we can get AIDS or other venereal diseases much more quickly; we can kill people from remote pilot-less drones. We can have anything we want at any time of the day. What a boon. The intimacy we believe we can increase which in the big picture leads to identity theft and affairs and even murder. The electronic fix: it promises so much and delivers so little. Sparks that rarely kindle fires.

So what do we do: we talk about everything and nothing. We text our souls into the oblivion of death or misunderstanding. It's a sitcom that turns out to be more annoying than comical. It's an infinite infomercial for something that can never be bought nor sold: contentedness.

Yes, it is true that one is not supposed to fall in love with one's therapist, but in this day and age, hasn't love been re-defined? How couldn't one not fall in love with a rental friend, she who is not a hooker, but a person paid to pretend to care and not offer advice but words that soothe? It's all about the soothing. A mind masseuse. For one hour in the therapy chamber, a hotel room of sorts, the most intimate details are shared and mulled over. Books, films, art are all discussed. The buzz one gets is something more powerful than any prescribed head meds. Then the time is up. So fast. It's extended speed dating at its best and the absolute ultimate is that there will be no sex. No sex. Ever.

It's on a higher level. A church between two. Souls interviewed.

She likes to read and suggests a library with the Babylon that surrounds and is the city. A place with books and films and a clean bathroom. A spot where Hemingway's old man from "A Clean, Well-Lighted Place" would feel comfortable if even for just a moment.

"Prince of the Tides" is the book she recommended and since it was written by a San Franciscan and is six hundred pages, it's more advantageous to rent the film, Depression tires the eyes in reading.

Barbara Streisand as the psychotherapist and Nick Notle as the beau. How perfect is that? No hidden message other than that of un-requited love and the gloomy sense of Romanticism it invokes– the guy who doesn't get the girl. In the end, there's an end. It's as simple as that. Ring around the rosie pocket full of posies, in the end, we all fall down.

We've been seeing each other for months, maybe even close to a year, and it feels like weeks. She takes trips to Scandinavia and the Caribbean and I ask about the details. About the taste of salty fish and how "conch" is really pronounced although I know it's "conk" and what she thought of those places compared to here. The here that looms outside of the window in its oppressive sunlight and green/yellow hills and buildings that look empty, like blocks of Legos, abandoned by children who have grown into melancholy versions of their parents.

She only tells the tiniest of details as I focus on a photo on the wall: a spider approaching the sweet spot of a flower. She took it herself.

Oh the verge of suicide only in the contemplative sense or utter madness due to the fact that I have burnt all my bridges that I've only ever constructed badly and hardly maintained during a life of little value to the outside world. Oh Bartelby if you could have only known what it feels like to have your disposition outlined by the muse of your own psyche. Oh Melville should I not say, how could you have made such a perfect candidate for Prozac?

Now don't get me wrong—it's not like I think about her when I'm not in her tiny office with a self-arrayed niche of knick knacks: the only ones I can remember are horses and the fact that she was born in Alaska. It's only when I'm with her do I sense a feeling of solidarity and that she gets where I'm coming from and that she too also knows she, we, the world and its denizens all have no cure.

As my own lack of progress is aligned to an identity crisis—a move to a big city, past the age of making friends (would that be around the early or late 20s?), I nevertheless take her advice to get on and into the world by attending a local fiction reading at a college just down the few hills I live within although I have no desire to hear or to be seen or to participate in the joy that is social interaction. Surely their stories of suffering cannot equal my own.

Death of father when I was nine, isolation from a large Catholic family as I was the youngest and most despised due to mother's attention for her little prince and a lifelong trail of missed opportunity due to the fact that making money or being successful has never been a goal of a lonely soul who sees no value in the ownership of material wealth.

So what is one to do with all the hours in a day? And how to admit to her, my confessor, that I am not what the world expects me to be and what I have been since the first day I slit my palm on a rusty slide at the park in which raccoons come out at night to invade the garbage can is a shadow. How does one casually tell another that they are a vampyre? In life: a loser. In the life of the mind: a psychic vampyre who feeds off others' auras, who nibbles at crumbles of others' souls. I am a shade and I feed of the energy of others. It is really that simple. I do not exist. The Hindus are right. This is all an illusion.

Ah the last confession. There is a forum out there of which we all know. A computer site I cannot mention by name or risk ridiculous litigation but allows me to say that it is very easy to procure a date.

And I am its daemon.

For fun this is what I do, somewhat professionally. I post an ad. Women, I assume, write to me. They are all the same: looking for prince charming, their other half. Some have had lives, have been married, have children they seek to in some way with me get away from, some have not. It's all so predictable and I guess that is what makes it so addictive . . . .

They always write the same things. I want this and this from a man, caring affectionate, must be tall, must have money. It's an a la carte menu of all they have forsaken in another in life for whatever reasons. They post terrible pictures that highlight their worst features: a crossed eye, to quote a jazz song a figure less than Greek, a hairdo from the early eighties, a shade of lipstick that is the color of Dead Sea mud.

And I prey on them like leach meal. I meet them at cafes or chain coffee houses. We talk of their hopes and aspirations and the pos- sibility that lies ahead. They tell me everything: about their last men, their sexual escapades, how their dreams were shattered, about deaths in the family and I drink it up like an elixir of misery that makes my skin feel electric. It is a hit of schadenfreude that I cannot resist and they want so little in return. An ear that listens, a touch of the hand, someone for once in their life to leave a gracious tip.

We meet, we measure each others' clothes, bodies, we indulge in fantasy and wonder, and we talk. They do not know I am soaking up their auras, drinking their energy, lapping up their desire and stress and angst. I tell them what they want to hear: how great I am in bed, how I love cleaning the house, that all children should be treated as if they were one's own. We laugh and joke and sometimes get a little tipsy. We share a cigarette. And then it's over.

Like the proverbial thief in the night I never contact them again. I become a void, the void that they carry within, the empty space that made them respond to my cleverly crafted ad, and they have only of me a memory. There are so many of these dispossessed souls why meet again? Ah, look at all the lonely people. How the Beatles were so right.

So how does this story end? It really never does. I could tell you that my therapist called, canceling our three o'clock. She has to attend a conference in St. Louis. Touché. I could tell you that she has broken my heart but I would be lying. I could tell you anything you wanted to know and like a fallen angel who just wants to say "I'm sorry" or "fuck you" one last time to his or her God, I will not be there or anywhere and you will feel the great emptiness in which we all live and where I reside. You too like me will become the silence that people drown in after reading a poem.

THE ATHEIST'S CLUB

Wanted: fellow small time philosopher/talkers to begin an informal discussion group. Call the Atheist's Club at 721-3487, leave a message.
—Classifieds, Sept. 199—

The Atheist Club met once a week, on Wednesdays, at three o'clock at the Airport Inn off of highway eighty. Highway 80 going west to better places like San Francisco, or, mostly, Reno. It was one of those places you would never stop at on the way to the airport. Unless you had a flat tire. Or you had to take a piss. Orange vinyl in the booths. Bauhaus light fixtures. Condom machines in the bathrooms. In the men's and the women's.

Thompson was the group leader. He chain smoked Vantages. It was more like he rope smoked; he'd have the next cigarette lit before the previous one was out. For a brief moment every few minutes, he'd have two grits lit up and unraveling in his mouth. Thirty-two, going bald, a manicured stubble on his diamond-shaped face.

Elise looked like she had it together. Tall, she always wore jeans that fit her perfectly, her mascara and lipstick were put on meticulously, could hardly tell her hair was once died blonde. She still curled her bangs, a habit hard to kick for some women.

Sometimes she would bring letters her friends sent and she'd read passages of them out loud to see the response of the others. Sometimes she'd pass them around so the stamps with their cancellation dates with the names of cities where they were mailed from could serve as proofs of their authenticity. She learned early on that the mail was never to be doubted.

Ernie Haifez was who he was. Never talked much, drank a lot of water, cleaned his fingernails obsessively. Four to five thoughts always going at once. He worked as a computer software jockey. Nobody knew exactly what he did with programs because no one exactly cared.

Myrna was a young girl. Twenty-two. Long black hair. A mole on her cheek. A matching one on the other. She was quite beautiful in a non-conventional way, a thing she thought she knew. Her hair shined, her lips were a certain shape; an ideogram for the pucker: insolent.

Stanton went to a podiatrist. He also had really white teeth, but no one ever complimented him on his smile. He worked as a secretary for a law firm. The pay was incredible, he barely had to work—some telephone calls, scheduling, lunches with the pretty assistant lawyers, that kind of stuff. He could eat donuts, drink coffee, and smoke in the front office. The view out the 15th story window was panoramic.

Helen was a vice-president of her father's bank. She drove a late model BMW, colored her hair with henna, and sang songs about her life when she lived in a small Indian town in northeast Arizona. After graduating from college, she taught in a sort of middle school on the reservation. She says, yes, she drank a lot and even had a few affairs.

Sometimes, they would stop their conversations to watch airplanes take off in 45 degree angles from the desert floor. Wings turning like arrows, then out and over the mountains and their snow covered spikes below. Nobody ever hoped they'd crash. Just what it would be like if it happened.

The resulting flames.

Normally, they would start off discussing what they'd been seeing on t.v. Some never watched television, but they read the papers and listened to radio. The media discussion got boring fast, and soon, sometimes too soon, the conversation would become personal. What they did during the week that was strange or so informative that they'd have to share it. This was how the locations of frequented dance clubs were divulged. Meetings, or get togethers, of a few of them at a local bar; the art movie theater or at Lucinda's, the latest non-gender specific hang out. Guys and guys and girls and guys and girls and girls, for a moment, getting together.

They'd talk about the drunk man who got arrested at a local art gallery. An opening of a new show of paintings by a former guard of a detainee camp once located not to far from the bustling downtown. The imbibed protester threw a glass of cheap California Merlot on one of the canvasses, and screamed, *touché, you builder of corridors*. Nobody knew what it meant.

Small talk.

When they got bored, they ordered food. Mashed potatoes and gravy was Myrna's favorite. Especially over a piece of bread and with some unclassifiable beef, like the kind they serve in frozen dinners. She also liked coleslaw and potato salad and apple pie, but ate these dishes very rarely and only when the club was convened.

Mostly everyone drank water, ate the ice cubes, had coffee, smoked, occasionally ordered a slice of cheesecake, and chewed gum. They would leave, awkwardly, when their throats began to ache and their eyes tainted red and their headaches started again.

They never discussed religion after the first meeting.

They did write a manifesto. It contained notations from the Christian mystics (all from Pauline Press editions), zodiac passages back-dated, random scribblings and not a few line drawings, lines of poetry remembered from high school, maps of unknown places, mostly in Europe, travel guide by-lines and interruptions from the news.

On this day of February the fourteenth, sacred day of the upturned phallicrum, the heart transposed, we adjourn the first official documentation of the league of non-theistic thinkers devoted to the free use of speech and undesignated time to gathering of trinkets of knowledge that are hopelessly nostalgic, in an unreasonably inept reportage, colored by the daily metropolitan frequency. . .

And so on.

There are some things in life you don't want to know about other people. They all discovered this quickly. Like shoe sizes. Ernie's is twelve. Helen used to beat her dog. Said it was the only fun thing she ever did as a child.

She'd been married four times. Her exes all pay her alimony, which she lived off of and part-time modeling before settling down in her family-given job. She even did some behind the camera fashion photography. Her dream is to live on a beach in Southern California and drink professionally.

Some things you do want to know about people. Like the fact that Myrna's mother is related to Valentino. This is where she says she gets her moles and black hair. Her mom is a designing consultant in the movie business, well, now mostly the television business. Her mom's the one who makes sitcom houses look lived-in.

Myrna lives in an upstairs apartment downtown. She keeps a cat and a bowl of goldfish. She says the place gets great light.

Thompson is an amateur race car driver. He's gone out a few times with Stanton to the abandoned airport to show his friend how fast he could go. Stanton said they never hit 120 mph, but the smile on Thompson's face and the whiteness of his hands on the wheel was worth the trip. The car: a 1968 Chevrolet Camero.

This never impressed Helen.

Ernie and Elise have been not exactly what one would call dating, but seeing each other outside of the club's meetings. They both liked to hike and are closet naturalists. Thompson said he'd seen them at the city park wearing backpacks, shorts, headbands; that they looked like matching activity dolls. He said that Elise's shirt was soaked wet with sweat but he didn't say that you could see her bra underneath. Thompson usually starts candid discussions before everyone arrives.

The story of Thompson was that he was married twice. In twenty-eight years. His weakness wasn't women, as Helen accused, but being with women officially. He liked pomp and circumstance: formal dining, ballroom dancing (he was taking lessons at Arthur Murray's). His favorite musician is still Chet Baker.

At the second convening, they all agreed to a non-dating clause. Except for the Ernie/Elise rendezvous, it seemed to be holding. Stanton surmised the mutual interest of those two had something to do with both their names beginning with an E.

Tonight was the group's fourteenth meeting. July 9th, 199-. They were becoming tired of discussing the news of the day and relaying their mild psychological discomforts and criticisms of the cost of living, high rents, no really hospitable bars in which to hang out, the tax rate, etc., so they decided to change their venue to that of a picnic. They'd meet next Wednesday afternoon at the lake. At the head of the lake, there was a hot spring where they could restore their powers of discussion. The club, based on believing in nothing and embodying it with innuendo-less gossip, was after six meetings running out of steam.

If the club was disbanded, it would only make their lives that much emptier. It was a looming possibility of which they all were constantly aware.

Wednesday was a beautiful day. The clouds were fair weather cumulus. They rented a van. Of course Thompson drove; he picked everyone up. Helen, Ernie, and Elise enthusiastically took the day off work. They seemed to be the ones most excited about the excursion. Myrna was wearing jeans and a halter top, carrying a bag of things she might need as the van wheeled into her driveway. Stanton saw her wave from her window so he reached over and beeped the horn, twice.

They drove the freeways of the city in silence and began talking only when the nothingness outside of the city forced them to.

Ernie knew of a clearing, surrounded by cottonwoods, not far from the lip of the lake. A path lead through a marsh to hot springs. There was a rock encircled fire pit nearby. He put a huge blanket on the ground, tacking it down with some stones and the cooler filled with beer. Helen brought three bottles of wine, one for herself, and two for the others. Almost as she exited the van, Elise threw off her shirt, kicked off her sweat pants and ran for the water. She entered with a calculated splash.

Thompson lamented the fact that he forgot his fishing pole. Stanton reminded him they were out to have fun.

They lounged on the blanket which was made of an indeterminable textile and was beginning to heat up in the mid-day sun. Myrna went for a walk. She was wearing hiking boots. Stanton disrobed to reveal a speedo. Helen remarked that he must also go to a pedicurist. His toenails were perfect.

Thompson was the next to go in. Elise was screaming at the others to join her. The water was frigid, but there were warm spots. Ernie followed, then Stanton waded in.

Helen surprised them all. Since there wasn't any others in sight for miles, she removed her shirt, with nothing underneath, and then took off her pants. She was wearing a bikini bottom. She walked into the water and broke into an olympic stroke at an olympic pace. Nobody commented.

Myna came back from her hike. She slowly took off her jeans and top. She had on a black one-piece and she put a pair of old tennis shoes on. She said she didn't want to step on anything alive.

The water was a force of buoyancy. They treaded in a constellation of each other and talked. This was a good idea, they agreed. After an hour of going under the murky water and floating above warm underwater springs, they got out one by one. Ernie was the first. The rest had forgotten that Helen was topless.

When she floated to the shore and pushed herself up, Myrna was the only one to stare at Helen's white breasts. The men, attempting to be European, casually disregarded the sight. Catching a glimpse out of the corner of his eye, Thompson noticed that her nipples were tense and reddened by the water. She put on her shirt in no particular hurry.

Elise had made a rice salad. Ernie brought some bread and goat cheese. They ate off of plastic plates and opened the bottles of wine. Myrna had a beer. Stanton began singing camp songs he learned as a Boy Scout. But the sun's rays on the water, the diminishing mountains in the distance, provided the real entertainment.

After eating and relaxing to the point where Helen almost had to be woken up, they decided to go to the hot springs. Shoes were required, the path was muddy and surrounded by eight foot weeds and marsh grass. Thompson led the way. Elise and Ernie were looking for birds, wondering how far away the springs were.

The path ran them through a labyrinth of possibilities of other paths. There were no signs. Stanton began whistling. Myrna trudged along in her sloshing tennis shoes.

After a mile and a half, Thompson found a dark pool surrounded by boards. Someone had built a sort of a deck out of shipping crates around a swimming pool sized hole in the ground that bubbled and churned. The smell of sulfur convinced them that this was it.

Stanton got in first. He said the water was scalding, but comfortably so. All you could see was his head smiling, eyes closed.

So what was nudity among a group of atheists Elise wondered to herself? This was one of those telling moments. Stanton said the water was very muddy and sandy; Elise didn't want to ruin her suit. With her back turned to the other she undid her swimsuit in two graceful movements and jumped in.

Ernie did the same, almost tripping out of his shorts. Thompson followed, saying, *when in Rome . . .* Helen took off her t-shirt, then slid off her bikini, then placed her glasses on her clothes. *The water is exquisite* she tried to convince Myrna, who was a little more than reluctant to get in.

Everyone found a place in the pool. Elise began to float, the tips of her pink toes breaking the water. Much wasn't said other than, this is great, this is wonderful. The temperature of the water modulated from hot to warm.

Myrna walked behind a stalk of vegetation and began sliding off her suit. She averted her eyes and calmly walked to the edge of the pool. She had a foot long scar across her stomach that the others tried not to notice. She had hardly any pubic hair.

They laughed and talked of becoming naturalists, of starting a nude beach here, and how they hoped no one else would by chance show up.

After a half an hour of soaking, Myrna was the first to get out. She said she was getting dizzy, drained by the heat. Sweat was beading on her forehead. Thompson got out to help her. A stream of sand ran down his back, around the curve of his butt, and down his legs. Stanton, said Thompson, you do have a nice ass. He got a towel for Myrna so she could exit privately. She nodded and put her hand on his shoulder, pulling herself out. It left a print in white.

The atheist club disbanded two weeks later.

They had said all there was to say. Their excursion to the hot springs couldn't be topped, or, as everyone knew, repeated. Rumor had it that Ernie and Elise were now officially dating. Helen routinely visited the lake by herself, half-hoping Stanton, or Myrna, or even Thompson might be there.

Stanton kept his secretarial job and began an affair with one of the Injury lawyers. Her name: Susan.

Thompson began to enter amateur car races, his racing car sponsored by the advertising firm for which he worked. He crashed in his second outing, dislocated his shoulder, and broke his tibia. Half of the atheists visited him in the hospital.

Myrna began taking classes at the university: Beginning Drawing and Life Studies.

Helen took out a loan, a major one, and began her own modeling and interior decorating business. It went bankrupt in six months. Her BMW, license plate number MDL 876, was seen leaving the city on interstate 80 on April thirty first. Her last meal in the state was at the Airport Inn. The waitress said she left a twenty dollar tip.

Her whereabouts, at this time, as most of ours are: (   ).

indian summer

AFTERMATH

Bad wallpaper, an interwoven bizzarity of fleur-de-lis and floral what nots, peeling in the corners, finger denuded light switch, unable to conceal cracks in the walls. It used to be a salon, when people did that kind of thing, met and talked and used the china that is now in boxes under the stairs. And smoked enough to cover the white ceiling with a thin paste of gray, impossible to ever scrub away. Decades of inhabited years passed by, inconsequential guests who worked, put up with unbearable jobs, ate lengthy meals, watched t.v. shows that still hang around in reruns, and fucked quietly and sincerely, as to not disturb the neighbors.

Funny how the years change the same way. The amazement in rain, especially how it darkens buildings and makes them look new, freshly painted, and as ancient as Roman bridges. Money put in the bank stays the same. Blood from a finger nicked on a broken window that looks out onto the street where people are walking, talking, holding leashed dogs soon to leave shit sculptures on the sidewalk. They are carrying loaves of fresh bread with the tips ripped off, eaten. Flowers grow in the cracks waiting the fluttering visitations of bees or the prying fingers of an interested child.

In the room whose doors don't exactly close square, some furniture remains that has been molded into the bodies that shaped it. A crooked chair with a leg in the air about to take a step, a broken vase undetectably glued back together, an obsolete fireplace, and a bed with no spine. The light fixture worked, if there wasn't too much humidity, with a crackle of energy that was either an assurance of competence or a warning of things to come. Next to the bed, an ashtray. A radio that still picked up a few stations, a mock-oriental rug with as much dog and human hair as fibers, and tiles that could be picked up from the floor, perhaps a forgotten idea to hide something valuable. A will willed, or emergency bus tickets.

In the late afternoon light, the few photographs taped to the walls, behind the door, one bare on a bare wall, and one close to the radiator, read as glares. These were the only clues. Minutes nearing an hour would have to pass before the pictures they portrayed could be viewed. They were just ordinary photographs, unframed, processed by some rinky-dink photo lab, and strategically placed with scotch-taped backs.

PHOTO OF THE BEACH

It couldn't have been anywhere, this was obvious in the long stretch of blue mountains tiptoeing into sea, a piece of machinery that could be either an ancient Ferris wheel or an oil pump (chain link fence surrounding), consistent line of garbage cans full of too much garbage, too many garbage cans in the world anyway, cloudy winter skies, the absence of people on the tan-yellowish sand. A white residue of slowly breaking waves shoreward, jeep tracks paralleling the water which was a gradation of sky. In the distance bright buildings, a suggestion of high rises petering out, a lot of blatant space, emptiness, seagulls.

Some people who maybe didn't want to be there, fists clenched tight and outlined in the pockets of their windbreakers. A few Mexican boys throwing a bouncing rubber ball against a wooden wall that separated the dining terrace of a cheap seafood restaurant from the rest of the recently rained-on pier. Bright painted pictures of seafood, crabs and other shellfish, with their names in English and probably, Chinese? It was break time for the bums. That is, when they got up and walked around and did what bums do– talk wantonly in a kind of logic no one understands. One such was in the restaurant conning the cook out of the old food about to be thrown away, guarding some donated fish fillets in a bundle of wax paper and sneering at gawking passersby. Eating lunch alone, sitting on the ground, with his legs dangling over the edge, above the nothingness of water and barnacles below. Happy.

There were couples too, holding hands and smiling to each other, taking in the sea smell and gray weather, thinking it was a day worth walking around. Couples in love with the thought of being in love and proving it by simply being together and not alone.

Old movie actors roamed this terminus of the great city reflecting on their bit parts in B flicks and runs in briefly known t.v. shows.

They wore jogging suits and thick- rimmed sunglasses to obscure their identities even further; they smoked and continue to smoke 100s, listening to portable cd players playing the current number one hit. Their big, expensive cars parked far away. They carried their *card* in their wallets, went about town to get glossies made, ate in three-star bars that served better drinks than food, had affairs with young want-to-be hopefuls who drifted in and out of town like returning swallows. The good life.

PHOTO OF A WHITE PARLOR, HEADLESS VENUS OUT FRONT

This beach, this pier, this mountainland drowning into a dull clouded sea offered everything a dreamer could want. Belinda—her real name— set up a tarot card reading business only two blocks away. She always had customers. Half tourists, half locals. All in desperate need of what was going to happen, if things would turn out because, even if you couldn't tell, everything was wrong. But it didn't look that way beneath the colorful clothes, the technically designed make-up, the fluorescent painted buildings and storefronts, the palm trees, a sea haze with an aftertaste of prozac, and pizza joints on every corner.

Now in her fifties, she had to run down to the convenient mart once a week to buy lipstick. Her bout of herpes would occur when the weather became cool, pinned like a pink carnation to her lower lip, yet conceal-able with the right amount of red. She painted her fingernails brown and read Tarot while chewing gum and tapping her feet under the table. The radio in her two-room bungalow, where she also lived, was usually on, inaudibly. The futures she constructed for her customers derived from her life as a singer in a jazz fusion band and her family history that included more abuse and abandonment than one human ever needs, more abortions than she cared to remember, a stint as a low-paid escort, and three marriages, two divorces. Her astral paths were well ingrained in the lines around her eyes and forehead.

When he entered her parlor, no appointment ever necessary, she thought she recognized him. Even he didn't know who he was. His purpose was simple enough. Still a young man, early thirties, he came to this particular part of the world to make films or be a screen writer, at the age and in the mindset in which dreams are still believable, but today he couldn't write or bear talking to another agent, so went to get his future read, perhaps to make it, in itself, a treatment.

Belinda was past the point of dreaming anymore, but not in believing in luck, especially since she found, at the flea market, a pack of Gypsy tarot cards with instructions printed in German, Croatian, Italian, French, and Hungarian. She said *hello* to him, asked if he would like a cup of tea, to which he said *yes, indeed*, pulled off his sunglasses bought from a drugstore in Venice Beach, to reveal his lucid green eyes under two thin feathers of eyebrows. He put two cubes of brown sugar in his cup, cut the cards, and watched her wrinkled fingers eagerly turn over the row of nine cards spread out before him. On the wall, he recognized an oriental rug hanging up slightly crooked, one he thought almost worth buying from the man who sold them out of his van down the street, on the corner where the gas station used to be.

The first card was Anger, *dispiacere* in Italian, and showed an old man with an English driving cap on his head and an apron around his body yelling at a boy in knickers who was apparently in the process of dancing. In the room in which the figures were, the door was open and there was a painting—a landscape—on the wall.

The second card was the Enemy, *feind* in German, a man in black in an alley of a stone city with a cane in his hand. He had a mustache, had one hand in his pocket, and seemed to be very cold.

The third was Malady, almost the same in French, a woman in bed with a medicine bottle, spoon in glass, on her night stand. Her body was covered up to her shoulders. The sheets brilliantly white.

The fourth was Gift: a red curtain, Spanish hand fan unfurled, two roses in a vase, a three-pronged candelabra, a jewelry box with the tail of a necklace protruding, tucked underneath it, a book.

The fifth was Merriment with a man and woman dancing under paper lanterns. The woman's face looked like a man's; the man's a woman's; shadows of trees obscuring the background.

Sixth card: Thought. A man in Victorian clothes on a park bench, legs extended, his finger parting the pages of a notebook on his lap. His environs might have been a park, but by the looks of the white stone bench he propped himself upon: a cemetery.

Seventh card: Unexpected Joy; joy being Freude in German, varatlan orom in Hungarian, and again, a man in top hat and bow tie in the northern countryside holding a portfolio and standing over a bag of money and a treasure chest full of yellow objects. In the distance: red steeples.

The eighth card was expectedly Death, who knows how it sounded in Croatian, smrt, a one-armed skeleton in robes holding an hourglass with all of the sand in the top chamber. The interior, a bare tree, a barren plain, a black horizon.

Last card read: Sehnsucht, ceznja, bramosia, vagy, désire—desire. A woman, of course, back turned to the viewer, parting the curtains to her room, in a red dress with a black sash around her waist, looking out into the orange/yellow beyond, other hand on her hip, on the floor an ottoman.

Belinda asked the man if the reading pleased him. When he shrugged, she leaned her arms on the table, pinched her chin, licked the two long rows of her teeth, and waited for him to ask her what it meant. Quickly, he put his sunglasses back on the frame of his skull, threw a twenty dollar bill in her direction. The wind from the open door he left behind blew the cards, and the one doily, off the table.

PHOTO OF FOUR FRIENDS

There are four of them, four people sitting on the steps. The house is beautiful, large bay windows, white columns, an oval window in the door, two big bay windows on either side. Him, her, her, and him. They are smiling. Real smiles, the kind that close the eyes.

They have just listened to a story, told by one of the women, that included the elements of an apartment in New York, a bathroom door, a negligee tainted with perfume, a married man, and hope. The men are not astonished and the other woman finds the story to be a somewhat modest vagary.

Later this day, the friends will take a ride above the city, to a park that overlooks a beautiful view and a hazy suggestion of a lake. They will look at the monument constructed there with some interest, speak of what books they are reading, walk a bit, and pretend they are happy in what one of them, the oldest male, previously referred to as the current "stations of their lives". The woman who told the story will reveal, as an aside, and by enacting it, that she has a slight limp.

The other woman, during their conversation on the porch and throughout the drive and stroll, thinks of a certain bird that she saw this morning perched on the wrought iron fence of the cemetery. She doesn't know the name of the bird and this bothers her but she doesn't think to voice her trifle. She will try to first sketch it in a notebook, then paint it using watercolors given to her by her daughter when she returns to her home.

The younger man, lost in polite solitude during the outing, wonders what the photo of him and his friends will turn out to reveal. He had set the camera on a garbage can and let it take the scene automatically. When the pictures are processed, he will notice pinpoints of light filtered through the tree branches that illuminate random areas of their gathering: stains of white on his knees, on the shoulder of his older male friend, on the cuff of the woman who told the story. The other woman, he notices, is holding a stamped letter that is eager to be mailed. She is seated in shadow.

They all correspond with each other and write their opinions freely on the page but when they are together, they talk to one another in pairs or groups of three. They know each other well enough not to pry into the realm of personal, private affairs, but reveal stories of their own lives at these rare intervals. What they learn about each other is what they already know about themselves: life is a complex unraveling of events never wholly understood but always worth discussion over a few glasses of good wine.

PHOTO OF AN ANONYMOUS WOMAN

She has ponytails and brown eyes, she is captured from the torso up. She is wearing a tank-top, one shoulder strap is pulled down midway on her arm. Her hand grasps the left top corner of her top. She is exposing her breast.

No one knows who she is, or rather, she knows no one who might be regarding her at the moment, because the picture wasn't merely taken, a slight crime in itself to stop reality in a pinprick of time and crop it into a portable square, the photograph itself was stolen. It was last seen, or displayed, in a house abandoned by previous renters and apparently clean enough and voided of existence to be shown to new ones. Except for this one souvenir. The question of its existence remaining might be answered by forgetfulness, perhaps it was left behind. Or it was left behind purposefully, as purposefully as the pair of tennis shoes remaining near the side door of the house. The house that used to be used as an office to rent spaces at the nearby mortuary that was styled as a Spanish villa. Who would want to live in such a place anyway, in plain sight of the apartments of death, another unanswered question. Yet there was the *For Rent* sign and a phone number written in heavy black marker in the front yard. A beautifully groomed lawn that directly led into the mortuary on one side and, separated by a low fence, an actual graveyard on the other.

Why this one item was taken by a prospective renter then probably used as a postcard mailed to an unsuspecting addressee is another mystery. Why it is again hanging to be viewed is as obvious as the day. The gesture is simple enough, release, the energy of encapsulation let free. A surprise. Freedom. Mardi Gras in New Orleans or the famous painting of the French Revolution, for precedence.

Its function in the room in which it is hung is that of a clock's, something to turn to when the moment of boredom strikes. A familiar unknown face who is alive, or was, breathed the different season's air, made soup from leaks and potatoes, brushed her hair routinely, was really loved by at least two of her many lovers.

Cities like the one the room is part of that the process is unending, universal, magnetic, vivifying, constant as the nightly illumination of street lights. In so many apartments built upon each other, houses orderly and square surrounded by the geometries of houses, office

185

buildings, bungalows in rows, duplexes and triplexes, that at any given time of the day, dawn, night, or evening, people are fucking. While one man waits at the dentist's office to get a check up, reading the dull magazines that pile up on a table no one ever dusts, above him, in a fifth floor apartment, people are fucking. Her hands are on his chest, the radio is on, both of their eyes are closed.

While she hurries into the grocery store with a list of items needed for a sudden dinner party, cracking a heel as she enters the store but not breaking it, in the van parked in the very last, further most parking place, they are at it. He holds her from behind, his hands on her stomach and she hold the muscles of his outer thighs. Their arms, interlocked.

As the distance-separated family waits at the airport for a sister to return home where she will perhaps stay to find a job and live, perhaps only arrive to visit and depart again, in the hotel across the plaza two people who barley know each other are fucking. She opens her legs to him, he stands at the edge of the high hotel bed, their hands clasped, as they unite their being, one to another, without words.

At the bus stop, three older women chat about the rising cost of vegetables. In the house behind, a married pair shower together, and carefully, as they are in a tub, he holds her as she climbs on him, and they join their bodies, in water and foam.

As the bomb in the metro explodes and anonymous people suffer the pain of ruptured eardrums and the inhalation of smoke, then are carted away to meet with first, doctors, then, police—lovers in an underground apartment bend over each other in the atmosphere of a shared bed, first her way, then his, for brief seconds, to obliterate time.

From within the room where the only clue to an existence is a few photographs, the sound of sirens are heard. The wailing sound of sirens resound and respond. There is no one in the room at the moment, but there will be. It is a city. There are always people. There always have been. There always will be. And the sound of sirens. Sirens, sirens.

THE EROTIC LIFE OF A DOG

for Kodiak

Darkness. But not really darkness, because in nearly dawn light, everything can be seen. A shoe under the bed. Goldfish not moving in their bowl and the water is calm. A drowned gnat lies on the surface. Bone near the mattress almost all chewed up. Maybe it'll be a good day. Maybe we'll go somewhere different. Different places mean different smells.

The cover is moving. So is the bed. They are breathing, but it's not a heavy sleep-breathing. They are breathing in each other's face and their eyes are not open. They are almost running and yet their feet, bare, sticking out from where the cover won't cover, aren't running. They are barely-moving feet. Tense feet. Even for a moment, curled feet.

Maybe this means we'll get up early. They are acting like they are eating something. There is no scent of food, in a way. There is musk coming from the bed, from their mouths, from their warm heads of hair, from their backs and from inside their bodies. They are not angry, or scared, or in pain, or in danger, even if they sound, and are making, scary noise.

If they could stop, or quiet down, to not make me wake up, they would. They can't though. They are past a point. One of their hands is grabbing at what it can. The hand is violent but not its gesture. The movement suggests it wants help, or more, of what it has. It will never have enough. This is well known. It comes with running, play, dinner, being touched, caresses, warm air after rain, or when someone returns.

What they are doing is not for everyone. Sometimes they change and continue. And change and continue. Sometimes the bed makes a movement or movements that are loud. Sometimes the bed really moves. When they are loud, it doesn't mean anything bad. This has to be learned. It's not easy. It's confusing.

When it's over with, they are happy. They are tired. They seem to like me more.

Days that we are walking a lot are best. Plants that you can eat and that calm the stomach, grow out of walls. The way to the beach and park is made of many, many smells: others, food, maybe cats hiding, many plants. They grow out of the ground where we walk. When we stop by doors sometimes they go in and I wait even though I don't want to wait. It is a garden that no one sees.

Then there are doors. I see them in a room behind the doors because the wall is made of what-looks-like-you-can-go-through, but can't. From underneath the door, foods that I do not normally eat, if any– small pieces of, spill out. Smells are taste. I know spill because it is what I do each time I drink water, but water is not the only thing I drink, sometimes milk. When they let me.

This food is good and they must wait to get it and they speak to another who is giving them the food. If they had tails they would wag. They say I am good because I did not run away, which they don't even know is a possibility, because there is food in the windows that I can see and I watch and I wait for it. There's always the chance of food falling.

When we walk far, we go to the beach—a place I didn't like at first because it was so big and I was young. On the beach many others go, many others like me even, and I meet them there and we run and we greet. Sometimes we pretend we are in love and are just acting like it, there is not much else to do and that is always fun. We take sticks and we almost eat them because they are like bones with no middles and we find rocks and chase them when they are rolling when they are thrown when they are like animals that we would like to kill. It's fun to pretend to kill!

To catch is fun too. We all like to catch, even bugs. Bugs bug us because they can hurt and go into us and give us sickness so we kill them. After we greet and greet each other again and run (it is like what birds do) we rest and we watch for smells. It's true and it is hard to explain but when we are out, and others like us—we can see and smell and sense what is not really there.

At the beach sometimes I see what's moving under water. We run we play we go into the wind that is part of us now, part of our hair. We are free, with out a rope. We are wild. We do not ever want to go back home.

Until it is time to go home.

Even, at times, when the people aren't looking, we go to the trees.

Once, while waiting in the kitchen, for the big yellow bowl, the one that means FOOD, it started to happen. She was there making the food, however it is made, because I never see the kill, or the cleaning, it just happens. It just appears. And there is blood. Sometimes there is some blood.

She was there making it, like she usually does. He was there too, doing something with a place where water comes. It was something that did not smell real, but smelled perhaps like flowers, and with what the food comes on, with them. There is cold water and there is hot water involved.

And she put her hands in the food and he came over to her. And he put his hands in the food. Then he put his hands on her, putting food on her! And she put her hands again into the food, food being made, food not food yet, and put her hands on him. But then they stopped to take off the hair that they put on them. They threw those them-smelling things into the corner where I usually sit, and they know this, and one of those went on my head, and on my eyes, and I couldn't see.

This was causing hunger to me, because it was food, and they were taking the food and putting it low on them, on them where I can reach with only my nose, and putting food there. They were eating the food. Maybe they were eating each other, just playing, but with food. Food on them!

And then they stopped.

Then they gave me food. But my dinner.

I was tired, after.

It's another morning, but it is a different one, because I can tell when they are different. Maybe not in a good way—they are putting me in water, warm and with something which smells. It smells like not-flowers. I am not sure if I like this—I am clean enough for myself—and even like they way my fur feels and is. This is their idea and it pleases them so I go through with it. Afterwards, I will fall asleep wrapped in clothes that I have learned the word for. It is "towels".

Even though it's a special morning they were at it again, I looked through the door they try to make closed by putting a rock near it, on the ground. But I heard and then I saw what they were doing, this time to music that was loud, I could hear them behind it, under the sounds. They do this and it is wild—it is like hitting—and then they yell at me and tell me no when I try to come in the room or when I go to others when we are walking on the streets and always at the beach (there are so many beautiful others). Don't understand. Don't even try.

It makes my legs shake. It makes me restless. It makes me think things. It makes me think of what would happen if I bit them. It makes me think of biting them where I shouldn't bite them: under the mouth. It makes me think that if I bite them under the mouth how it would taste, how it would feel, to feel moving in my mouth. It makes me think of blood and how blood tastes when something is moving in my mouth and I am feeling the blood taste. Blood, muscle. Meat. Veins. Ropes of skin. How I like to tear.

Bones are just as good. From time to time, I get one. For what, I don't know. Maybe so I don't kill. Cats, especially.

They are everywhere here, cats. In trees, or always ending up there, on fences. They rest on cars, they sleep in bushes, they sit on benches as if they were people and they wait until old women feed them. Some in the woods within the city live in trees and they sometimes have only one eye or an ear or even a tail missing. What pain they must go through to live where they do.

They are nobody's cats and they know it.

I chase them for fun. Not really wanting to hurt them, because they have wounds. Licked and healed wounds. I don't want to catch them or eat them or even bite them, I want just to chase. A chase might mean a catch or maybe it won't fight and it will want to be my friend. Friend or foe is the rule. Many people don't seem to understand this.

I can hold my own. Against any other dog or cat. Even horses don't scare me. Except their feet.

Cats are not a problem. What they do that no one likes is eat all the fallen food on the streets. Nothing left for us, then. And cats, they eat everything: bones, meat, insides, outsides, and they clean the ground with their horrible tongues.

There are really not many problems being me. Storms are not good. When it's too wet and cold comes wet and makes heavy my fur and falling water is cleaning everything and the smells off them and loud noises from above that can't be seen—that is especially not good.

Loud noises mean trouble. They excite me.

For the moment, I am happy. I enjoy wagging my tail and keeping it wagged. I sleep a lot. I find things, mostly rocks, in the ground. That I can find things is good. That the beach always has sand and water is good. That there are sticks and cats and dogs, good. Seasons and wind and sleeping in moonlight. Climbing up the stairs when there is the smell of food. Puddles of water not to wash in.

Spilling my water on anything that smells real. Real with the piss of others.

Piss tells me everything I need to know.

Going away and coming is what I don't understand. Sometimes they are gone and sometimes they return. When they go, I don't like it. I must wait. I don't know where they are. I can't watch them.

When they come, I am happy. It is great. It is the first time I see them. We might go out. Maybe we'll eat. It's just wonderful. When they go, where they go I don't know. There are so many different places beyond the door. Beach. Hills. Woods. Other houses. So many places I don't know.

They're at it again. This always happens. Maybe because it's spring. This time I'll act like I don't care. I'll pretend I'm sleeping. I'll pretend I don't see her going on top of him. I'll pretend I don't see him standing behind her. I'll pretend that they are not in pain, and that they don't need me (they do) and that they are not hungry for each other's flesh (they never break skin) and that it is not hurt they want.

In the way they breathe, there is heat. In the way they move there is danger. They are leaving themselves open to each other, both. Her legs are up in the air, where there is nothing to walk on. He is pushing himself into, where the rest of his body can't go. They are holding onto each other with such strength that red marks are on their bodies. Around handprints, blood is flowing. How blood flows.

Yet another day, and I do think they are forever, days, and I walk from room to room. Always watching them. If they are going to take me somewhere. If we are going to eat, the bigger one is always eating or drinking something. Sometimes he throws a bit to me and I catch it and I taste it and it is gone and I feel good. Looking in the corners where it is dark I can see small things moving. They are little bad creatures because they try to eat our food even if it is food in the bag I cannot go in, the bag to throw away.

In the afternoon sun, I dream of swimming, or bones, especially the perfumed bones of fish, I dream of food and of being wet, then getting dry, without actually doing it, really best that way. In sleep my legs run and I see lights and it is like being there, being awake, wherever I want to be, but not being there, like when birds leave the beach in a gust of wind and I chase them and I find water and for a minute with them I am swimmmmmmming—

FAMOUS LAST WORDS

The year we decided to kill ourselves was a beautiful year. It couldn't have been a better time. Really. Everything was going right. Life couldn't have been better.

Mornings began with a bright, almost bone-white sun. We lived in a quiet, historic neighborhood in anytown U.S.A. and our neighbors were nice. Sometimes they would even bring us food and talk to us about the flowers they were in the processes of planting. We would leave saucers of milk out for the stray cats so they wouldn't be strays in our yard. The oak tree that shaded the house was perfect for climbing. Sometimes we would sit in its branches and talk. We would watch the traffic drive by.

We had friends. They would visit and enjoy the meals we took hours to prepare. There was always enough wine. We would play music that we didn't particularly like, but knew they would. Since we were new to the city, so were our acquaintances, and with them we would talk about our past lives, recount the stories that defined our current selves, chat about how we were going to improve the house, what to do on weekends, the few restaurants we knew. Sometimes, we would go to a play or to the movies with them and sit silently together in the dark and wonder who the people were who sat around us and what the city would look like once we returned to the reality of the street lights and the monotony of background sounds. A fire truck speeding to a cloud of smoke as the sunset colored it and the sky pink.

In all directions, there were mountains. So many that it would take a lifetime to learn the names of them all. Or two lifetimes. We even climbed a few, not knowing then that we wouldn't have a lifetime to get to the thousands of different views of the city, to see the land outlying, to see the city from afar. Differing perspectives. To think it doesn't make sense, but in reality, our lives seemed like a dream.

The dream was to be there. And there was simply anywhere, where we were, together. A place with schools and churches and bakeries and bars and squares where people could go and meet to talk. We should have known that something was wrong when the city's few blocks of gridded downtown was empty at nine p.m. We should have known there was something wrong when for fun, kids would scale the few skyscrapers, really only tall buildings, and parachute off them for kicks. We should have known but we were living in a woken dream. And it was the kind of illusion that just makes sense. A kind of rational nightmare.

Hindsight views can be 20/20, but they're usually murky. Just ask the man floating face down in the pool in Sunset Boulevard. Through the antiseptic water, his life looks like something clean and preserved in amber, but it's not. It's a blur of tranquillity. It may be true that I didn't learn much in my brief tenure on Earth, but sight was one thing I had mastered. Because jobs were scarce, I worked as sort of a low grade private eye for a while. A commercial spy of sorts. The pay was good and it gave me a lot of time on my own. Time to look, watch, and listen. It was my job to see things other people routinely missed. You'd be surprised at how often people touch, say their nostrils or private parts, in the course of a day.

The first place the temporary agency sent me to was a bookstore. It specialized in stacks and stacks of rare and ancient books. The guy who ran the store was a true bibliophile. He was retired from the insurance business and sank all his money into acquiring first editions of books on Western Americana. He had people working for him all over the country—sending him books, magazines, broadsides, monographs that he really only wanted to display. If he liked the customer, he might maybe sell.

Probably more out of paranoia and bad record keeping than fact, he thought people were stealing from his shelves, so he hired me to pose as a browser and keep my eyes open. It wasn't hard work. A lot of standing and, to tell the truth, I didn't have an interest in cowboys or the West. In the hundreds of books I paged through, feigning interest, I can't recall one famous outlaw's name other than the best known. Jesse James. Read too much about the dental work of Butch Cassidy to even care to recount it.

You could so easily tell when someone was about to steal

something. It was consistent as time itself and as apparent as ritual. Just before a skinny adolescent put a book, or magazine, in his jacket, or her purse, they would look up twice, in two directions, to either side of them. This movement, what I called the *don't-look-at-me-I'm-stealing-something* twitch, made my job easier.

Now if thieves could only learn to not think about the act of thievery, to read the coveted object calmly, and without moving a head, or blinking the eyes, just tuck it under an arm and walk cleanly through the doors, my job would have been a challenge. It's in the unconscious act of re-enacting stealth that gives it all away.

Normally, the old coot wouldn't prosecute the would-be criminal, but we'd take him or her into a back room and threaten them and prohibit them from ever returning. The daily rush of being a predator stalking unknown prey kept the job interesting for the two months before I quit. I couldn't stand the smell of old books. Add the fact that Western Americana isn't the most coveted or resale-able merchandise under the desert sun. And the horrible music playing over the ceiling speakers.

My wife worked as a travel agent. I would drive her to work, fifteen miles through the guts of the city, where she would sit at a desk with a headset phone, and make reservations for people lucky enough to fly to Athens or London in the spring or Stuttgart for an art festival. Often, in between calling airlines, she would call me on my portable telephone, and in a quiet voice, tell me exactly how she wanted to have sex that night. Her descriptions were of an elaboration that only boredom can produce, including detailed descriptions of positions that were sometimes feasibly impossible, and play by play narratives of what most assuredly would occur. She would then abruptly hang up. In short, she made my lunch breaks ravenous.

It was too bad the nights never resulted in much. We were too tired to enact the fantasies of the mid-afternoon, too harried by the people we had to put up with during the day, to break out of our routine egos. There was always the next day and the possibility of its fantasies.

You see, we were badly in love. Not the kind that makes people stroll around the park holding hands or coming home on Valentine's

Day with a bunch of roses and a grocery store box of candy. We were forever on our third date. We still made out at the movies. We drove around the city looking for places to sit under trees, take our shoes off, roll cigarettes, and talk about the view. We wrote each other silly, nonsensical notes and left them about the house. We were always together, spending hours in the public library showing each other books, napping in the rows near a bright window, staying unmarried because an official bond would ruin it all. When we both quit our jobs to be alone more with ourselves, our friends though we were crazy. But we weren't insane, just lovesick.

When we couldn't make the rent anymore, we sold what we owned and moved into the basement of a colleague of mine. He was a lonely bachelor who had many city-wrought phobias such as going to the store, driving on crowded highways, attending Christmas parties, so we lived and worked as his life-assistants as he called it. We helped him with the practical aspects of existence and he learned from us something about the rarer side of life, intimacy and happiness. Illusions of a higher degree.

But three's a crowd. He began coming on to her and subtly insulting me by asking too many intimate questions. We couldn't live as slaves forever, we thought. We were slaves to ourselves, to the concept of each other. So we moved out and into a cheap hotel, more of a boarding house, in the downtown of the city none too far from the proverbial railroad tracks. The building-hotel we lived in was quite beautiful. It's architecture was from the late 1800s and the rooms were immaculate and huge. We could easily hang our laundry in ours and still have enough elbow and standing room to live normal lives. It only cost eighty dollars a week. We cooked on hot plates and sometimes went to the hotel cafe for morning coffee.

I even began helping out in the kitchen. There were hardly ever any guests so business was slow. Our specialty, that is, the hotel's, was barbecued ribs that weren't barbecued but heated up on an open air grill and smothered in store bought sauce, and hamburgers, a salad bar, and potato soup. This varied menu brought in the desperate just traveling through type and old people who didn't care what they ate as long as it was food during Sunday brunches.

The downtown in which we were situated was deader than a shore washed bird. It helps to remember that this city was a western metropolis, and there really isn't such a thing in the hard-line European sense. Buildings constructed on a sight absent of history will be just that, buildings, and not places. There were, to its credit, a couple of pool halls selling unreasonably priced beer and smokes, a few jazz or country-blues clubs with high hopes but not the billings, museums that only school children attended by force, and some open-air festivals that were mainly excuses to use new, well-oiled parking decks.

There was a valiant attempt at sculpture cropping up from time to time, corner to corner, on the sidewalks: bronze imitations of happy families, or children playing, in dark brown stasis. It was an unconscious salute to the fear of nuclear warfare—what it might look like at that last, terrible, unknowing moment. It was bizarre to see such a large city, complete with skyscrapers and foreign grocery stores have so little of a definition of itself.

In short, the possibilities were endless but the probabilities few.

It takes more than two to paint a town red, but we tried anyway. We sampled the restaurants, when money permitted—my beloved began teaching private lessons in Italian cooking to coteries of spinsters and a few young men freshly graduated from cuisine schools, so we had an minimal income that allowed us to exist with a modicum of happiness, if not style. We went out to bars, got drunk, and asked each other to dance We picnicked in the mountains, building fire pits to cook our free range chickens; we sang campfire songs and had wild sex holding onto trees for support, then condolence.

Happiness, exquisite happiness, is a joyous thing, yet when it's shared only between two, and not communicated to others, shared with a greater whole, however stupid this might sound, soon turns to loneliness, and left to ferment, can become a strong vintage of sadness.

The signs came like a comet stuck stationary in the sky. She began to become silent for long and frequent stretches of time. I would catch her, in her plush lounge chair that looked like it should be at an antique dealer's, just sitting and staring out the window. The window that held a view of the street that changed only with the seasons. Sometimes under her breath she would say, "Here come the garbage trucks."

I began looking for a steady job as a forest ranger. I thought it to be something I might want to do, even though it required month stays at stations far in the mountains and inter-mountain foothills. Perhaps time away from each other would enliven our moods. Living in a hotel gave us a deep recognition of the transitory nature of our coming together and being here, which really was nowhere, with no prospects for the future, except to grow older and to lose more of what little youth and happiness we already had.

We went mushroom hunting. I got some books on species and it was all too simple to find poisonous ones, especially after a rain storm. They popped up right under pine trees, unearthing a clump of dirt and the woven bed of needles.

In our hotel room for two, we cooked them in a pan with butter, white wine, crême-fraiche on a hot plate that I bought at the Salvation Army across the rail yard. It still had its price tag of 2$ on it. We had a candlelit dinner. We drank two very expensive bottles of wine and then went walking the empty downtown streets. It had just rained–the streets were wet and smelled of fresh dust and the traffic lights illumined them with eerie, late night light shows. We passed small restaurants and nightclubs that were reached by stairways going down, beneath the level of the sidewalk. They too glowed in a neon of the other world and were peopled only with a few stragglers who were hiding out from the now blown by rain clouds.

In the window of a bakery, we saw a gigantic wedding cake gaudy with frosting flowers. We passed a disco that had a poster of a embryo's head on the body of an armadillo. We walked by a Lebanese eatery filled with only the family that owned it, talking loudly and filling glasses with pitchers that were wet inside and out, with water. In the distance, winding through the square city streets, there was the rumbling of where the storm was going.

Nothing could help us now. We ate our last meal and the mushrooms were having a joyous effect. We spoke words that didn't even sound like words, and thought perhaps the variety of mushrooms we picked and cooked were simply hallucinogenic. I do not want to reveal the name and genus of them as they are all too easy to locate, and even in death, I fear responsibility.

Soon though, I began to burp, then upchuck a liquid, then begin vomiting a thin yellow string of liquid that seemed to contain either egg whites or snakeskins. It felt as though I could suck the fluid from my entire body into my stomach then lead it up through my throat, mouth and nose, with the utmost ease.

She began falling down at the crossroads and unwilling to get back up. I held her in my arms and tried to carry or drag her back to our home, our room in the hotel. She moaned and stroked my hair with the back of her hand.

My vision blurred, no not really, it sort of went out and the roar of passing cars sounded like the screams of airplanes taking off and crashing on the runway. To say that your life passes before your eyes is a lie. It's your death that traipses by with a slide presentation of all your friends and family, successes and failures, happy and sad events, in one long silent running commentary.

We both expired that night, in each other's arms, on the corner of Fairview Avenue and Ninth Street, looking into each other's eyes to the very last moment, a moment that felt as good and true and pleasing as an afternoon nap. A moment that took the place of a future we didn't know, a moment that lasted forever in eternity, lit by the flickering green red and yellow of traffic lights, our limp bodies collecting the stray thoughts of garbage in transit, our heartbeats as still as the wings of a moth in a closet.

We hope to be remembered.

LUCINDA

So there I was. Piece of shit freeway between the crummy town I lived in running to the even worse town in which I worked. The sun was burning bright, so bright it was blinding and maybe that was the reason no one was slowing down. Waving my arms like a madman, ok, maybe not the best way to solicit help, but when you're in a state of emergency, what else to you do? I felt like jumping out in front of an oncoming truck. There weren't any. And there weren't. There weren't. There wasn't anything.

Or, there were long periods of silence, broken by only the sound of a car coming—passing—departing—and an echo of my own gagging voice in full fledged curse. Screw all motorists! Where's their sense of fidelity, where's their feeling of brotherhood? That's what cars do to us, little coffins on wheels. They take us faster to the end.

The sun was burning bright. Real, real bright. Made brighter by surrounding fields of snow. Gullies frozen solid with ice. The freeway was white, with breezy drifts of snow, and dried up marshes where trucks dumped crystal loads of salt. Everything was white but nothing looked cold.

There I was. Should have known better than to go to work on a day that the high temperature was expected to be negative 20 even without the hedge of the wind chill thrown in. As a rule, you shouldn't be expected to DO anything on a day that the friggin sun isn't even working, a day that can't even get warm enough to get your blood pumping, your lungs up and popping, your brain stewed to the degree of coherent thought.

What a wonderful day it was to pick the scenic route to work—highway numero 12—cutting through beautiful loping hills of farmland and stands of poplars near the bridge where the river cut through and barren stretches of grazing land for horses and cows (who weren't stupid enough to be out) and rustic old farm houses and barns way off the highway looking like children's toys in the distance at the ends of frozen dirt roads with those dusty squirrels' tails extending from them to a mailbox and a name painted in big black letters.

I should have known that the rental car I was driving, no more no less than a 1981 Ford Escort, would break down the day the insurance company procured it for me. And what an escort it was: metallic blue with a red interior, the heat barely worked especially on a day like this, the radio picked up only religious stations and farm reports, there were no interior dash lights to speak of illuminating the driver's thoughts at night, and the biggest insult was the cigarette lighter that wasn't there but mocked you by providing in its absence a tiny cylindrical glowing cavern leading nowhere. Lighting nothing. I couldn't make a boy scout fire to keep my hands warm.

The car was majorly dead. A cracked crankcase or something big. It just lost power and coasted to its bitter, as in bitterly cold, end. It looked like a dead turtle on the beach of the highway's shoulder. I left it for death a half mile down the road.

It was so cold I could taste my breath, and it wasn't a flavor I would recommend. There are just those days when it's so bone chilling that all you can think is *god it is cold* and there are those days that start off so bad you can taste how much worse they will get on the back of your tongue and you can smell the awfulness of the oncoming day at the very back of your nostrils, almost underneath your eyes, and this is why some people drink liquor straight up—not because they like it like that, because it erases the misery that inhabits the air, your body, your hair, and all those musty spaces within and in between.

I knew that the bed and I should have not interrupted our platonic love affair.

But there I was, waving my hands at the relatively few cars on the desolate highway on a desolate winter's day and I could not believe that the seven, count 'em, 7, that drove on by me drove on by! I felt like an idiot ground crew member on an aircraft carrier on waters so rough the planes couldn't land, endlessly aborting. *Whizz*—another passes by as the cloud of my breath freezes in front of my face, for a moment. I would have begun crying at about rejection number four, but I knew the tears would only freeze and cause me sad clown tears of frostbite. At number six, I kicked my own foot. Didn't feel it.

Number seven I attempted to hit with a rock encrusted with ice and only lost my mitten.

Car number eight appeared to show the recognition of empathy by slowing down. The driver inside, wearing a ski mask, seemed to have made, or at least attempted, eye contact. He passed me and I let out a load and squelchy *F—Y O U*, and then saw his brake light blink on an illusory color of red I could barely see shining under the whiteness of snow and sun.

I shuffled up to the stopped vehicle, my joints barely functioning in the cold, its tailpipe coughing up water and threading out a stream of condensation. It was a family-sized vehicle, a sedan. The silhouette of a person inside was gesturing APPROACH from inside of a scraped off circle of frost and three day ice on the window. It appeared that the person was piloting his ship from four evenly sized portholes.

Outside the passenger's door I heard what I thought was a muffled "Get in!" I raised my mitt to the car door and distinctly heard, " . . . in back!"

The door opened to a pile of things, some being a balled up afghan, various half-folded up road maps, a small broom, a thermos with its lid unscrewed, a pair of nice dress shoes, some pink and yellow pieces of paper that looked like airplane tickets shorn of their protective folder.

"No one would stop for you?" the driver asked from behind a ski mask. It was a man's voice.

"Not a soul," I replied "you were the first to even think of slowing down."

"Unbelievable," he said "in this weather. You could have frozen to death."

"I know, I know. The car—it isn't even mine. It's a rental. A piece of crap."

"They all are this time of year. Where you going?"

"Anywhere in town, you can drop me off at the first intersection. That'd be fine."

"No problem, it's o.k. I'm just running errands, I can take you where you need to go, just let me know."

"Great, the car place is on Washington."

"Where's that?" he asked.

"On the way into downtown, past the Holiday Inn, not far."

"That's on my way, anyway." He seemed to be happy to offer a hand. He gripped the steering wheel with one hand and with the other tore off the navy blue wool ski mask. A long mane of light brown hair sparked in static electricity. He turned his head to me, in the back seat, smiled a sweaty smile.

"Hey man, you saved my life." I offered.

"It's nothing man, I do shit like that everyday."

I realized that I was sitting in the middle of his backseat, the only place made available by the pile of what every long distance traveler accumulates on the long boring highways of the country. My inadvertent position was made even more apparent by my bad habit of scanning a face caught in the unacknowledged portraiture of a rearview and his right eye catching me and winking me away. I looked down, in front of me, in the passenger's seat, and saw another bundle of stuff.

Under the bundle of stuff, which I took to be an outgrown winter's coat folded among yesterdays paper and a fast food lunch, was a baby seat. In the baby seat was a baby sleeping. On the floor of the passenger's side was more assorted junk, one of those coffee cup holders you hook onto the window, an ice scraper, and a casual collection of those tiny little liquor bottles you get on airplane trips. They had their tops off. They were empty.

The micro-climate of the car's interior didn't smell like booze though. And his eyes weren't glazed over. He stared intently on the sun brightened freeway, as if he were counting each yellow dash and accumulating this numerology for some reason in the depth of his mind, switching his view every so often only to glance at me in the back, and smile.

"So, you're from around these parts, huh?"

"Yep. I was just on my way to work. At least the car didn't die on me after a long day."

"Yeah, you're right about that" he assured me.

"Is that yours?" I motioned to the sleeping child with my head. Stupid question.

"Yeah, yeah. She's seven months. Apple of my eye. I'm from Denton. Know where that is?"

"Nope, never heard of it." I hadn't, or at least, had never cared to.

"Oh, it's about two and a half hours south of here, along the river. Not much of a place. But it provides me with a job, so I can't complain.

"Yeah," I said, "doing what?"

He looked out from behind the windshield, scanning the horizon as if he were expecting something. As a matter of rote, he checked all three rearviews, then sucked something through his teeth. "Paramedic."

The kid in the plastic seat began to squirm a little and make noises like a pig suckling. Like it was eating something or wanted to.

He pulled the blanket from its face, probably to keep it warm, and tucked it under its chin. Couldn't tell if it was a girl or boy, but there was no mistaking its resemblance to him.

"So I'm taking you downtown, right?" he asked? "Hey, you like music?"

"Yeah, sure." I was almost warm enough in the car for me to remove my gloves.

"What kind of music?"

"Oh, all kinds, you know rock, jazz . . ." I didn't want to divulge that maybe I wasn't a country-western fan.

He put the radio on to a jazz station. "Yeah, I dig jazz too. As long as it's classic jazz. Don't like this crappy elevator music stuff they call jazz, or smooth jazz, or whatever. There is no such thing."

"Amen to that." I added.

The nothingness that was empty farmfields and stretches of cropland with every so often a mechanic's shop in a quonset hut passed by quickly while we were trying to find things to say to each other. We passed a place that manufactured tombstones.

"Bet that place has a jumping showroom."

The funny thing is that I couldn't help myself from peering over the front seats' edge and looking at the baby all calm and quiet, wearing a little red winter cap with a big poofy white ball on it, just lying there not knowing what was going on. Not caring about cars, or jobs, or the winter, or problems, or life for that matter.

There were fifteen miles to go to get to the city. Only problem was that the road was iced-over in parts, so the going was slow. The radio was barely audible. He wasn't asking me what I did for work. Wasn't much to say. Gratefulness often recedes into silence.

"Yeah, I save people's lives all the time. I mean, it's my job and all. It's not like I can kick back and slack and let a few go, you know."

"I imagine not."

"I mean, I do it all the time. Do it so much that it even starts to get boring. Sometimes. I mean, it's all a matter of a pinprick, really. One second the blood's flowing, the lungs are pumping, heart's beating away in the dark cave of your chest, eyes are wet and moving, and in a pinprick, I'm talking a little teeny weeny sewing needle here, it can be shut off. Dead. Nothing. You'd hardly even notice it. Not at first anyway. Not until all the fluids settle. Not until the body starts getting rigid. It's like a clock. We're like clocks, just ticking away. If even any one of those vital gears or switches fail– hey, no more time."

The baby in the front seat writhed a little. I thought it strange that a man like he was, a paramedic, would put a kid in the front seat. But I didn't say anything.

"So do you see a lot of–"

He looked back at me.

"Death?" you mean.

"Yeah," I said, " . . . a lot of stopped clocks?"

We were slowly making our way into town. Gas stations, more than any city of twenty thousand ever needed, began clogging up the view from the steamed windows. People were running into the stations and then windsprinting back into their cars because it was so damn cold. People running in snow boots is a sight to see.

"You wouldn't believe the shit I see, I mean, for a small town."

"I bet."

"I mean, it'd surprise you."

"O.k., such as?" I asked because he seemed to be pursuing the topic.

" . . . well, of course there's a lot of kids with arms mangled by farm machinery, you know around here, even legs nearly chopped off, dangling by threads. There's the every so often gunshot wound or knife slash due to a 'misunderstanding' at a local watering hole. There's the every odd naked woman found in a drift of snow with no foul play or motive to indicate homicide. "Happens at least once every two years . . ."

"Really?"

"And, you know, there's the car crashes, the drunk drivers with their skulls cracked open, missing so much brain that there ain't nothing we can do. And there's burn victims, sometimes even profs at the university in the chemistry department who mix some kind of concoction and end up burning the whites out of their eyes . . ."

"No way . . ."

"But the weirdest, the strangest of all, is, well– can you guess?"

"Crimes of passion? Hits? Haven't heard of any maniac killers in the papers of recent," I was guessing.

"Suicides."

He said it again, this time nodding his head in a type of assurance, or knowledge, only he possessed.

"Suicides."

He smoothed back the hair on his deep-in-sleep child's head and flicked the turn signal on, entering town. There were hardly any cars on the streets. No one was going to risk it.

For a minute, I had nothing to say. Dread of those penny-ante procedures I would have to go through shortly to get myself out of this situation drained me of all inspiration. Yet I thought, out loud, "Why would a paramedic be called to a suicide scene?"

"'Cause," he said an air of superiority that came with a position in the life/death industry, "sometimes they don't get the job done. You see, there's always the chance that we can revive them, then . . .," he chuckled ". . . prosecute them for breaking the law."

"Oh yeah?"

"Suicide's a crime in these parts, you know."

206

The car stopped. We were at the intersection where I needed, or thought I did, to be dropped off. From there, I could see the river frozen over and small, step-shaped drifts of snow, resembling waves, or some kind of one dimensional staircase leading out to bare pools of black ice. For all that it'd be worth, all the sunshine of the day, it would be night by four thirty p.m.

The baby, sensing a lack of movement, began to fidget in its seat. And make a gurgling noise.

"There was this one guy . . ." he shook his head to himself and continued ". . .who did it by rigging up an elaborate yet home-made contraption: he soldered wires from his fillings, do you hear me, his *fillings* in his *mouth*, strung that into an electrical cord, like he cut it from a lamp or something, and plugged his face in the wall. Imagine the toothache!"

"You're shitting me."

"No way man, I was there. I won't go into the gory details, but, you should have smelled it in there."

I could, but didn't, imagine.

"Then there was this lady, and we don't know, the cops don't know, her family don't know, don't anyone know why she took this hedge clipper thing, you know one of those big saws, the kind that look like the nose of a saw fish, and she put it in her, if you know what I mean and she turned it on and she put it most of the way in her and those things are long, like real long—what?—about a foot and a half and when we got there I don't know why they even bothered to call us 'cause the pool of blood turned almost completely all of the white shag in that room into a brown carpeted room and you know what the forensic experts said, at least what the rumors were around the office the next week . . .?"

"No, I . . . can't even . . . imagine—"

That she died in a state of ecstasy. The best orgasm she had ever had.

"*Wa-wa-WAAAAAAAAAHH!!!*"

The baby started an all out cry.

I put my hand on the window and it felt like dry ice. I motioned towards the door and thanked him for the lift. I noticed that under his legs, on the driver's side floor, he had amassed a pile of pulled off rubber gloves. He noticed me noticing them and said, "Keep your hands real warm, here—want a pair?"

I said, "No, uh, no, can't stand they way rubber smells. Or feels."

"Oh."

"Thanks anyway, for everything."

The baby's crying picked up volume. It wanted to get humming on the road again, back into its thought-womb. Tears began to trickle down its pale face, leaving little warm trails of red and wetness.

"Yeah, just be careful out there, it's real cold. Driving a crummy car like yours on a day like today ain't real smart buddy."

"I know, I know, probably will have to go back and get it later, or tomorrow."

"Some might even say that driving out there in the middle of nowhere like that on a day like today is even a bit, well, death defying."

"Yeah." I pretended to laugh.

Last thing I heard was the sound of the baby gulping down its own tears and sniffling as I shut the door and he drove off, smiling and nodding his head. He waved to me again, and I wondered, I truly wondered, what was that beautiful child's name.

CONFESSIONS OF AN ALTAR BOY

Forgive me father for I have sinned and these are my sins.

Fucked up. I got fucked up. We got loaded. We got dizzy-eyed fucked up. We did it before every mass. This is a sin? We were the altar boys from Hell.

It was my doing, too. Or was it that swollen potato of Father L.'s nose that got me thinking? That huge, huge nose was all crosshatched by veins and shining in the dim lights of St. Vincent de Paul's church. Our church, our Temple of Amen was a flying football shape that we ourselves built with weekly contributions and out of poor mothers kitchens. Poor poor, sad sexless women who spent their time, extra time baking cookies and rice crispy treats, so their sons and daughters would get in good with the nuns. We kept oragami cardboard collection baskets in our homes, too. For spare change.

Like whose?

I asked Coogan why it was like that, his nose. Why it was so big. Like W.C. Fields'. Why he had a nose growing on his nose. Coogan said it was just like his Dad's—too much drink. Booze. Hootch.

So I got to thinking. Even before the wine is magically changed into the blood of Christ, it's wine. Ain't it? Pretty good stuff too, by looks of the label. Some words I couldn't understand, but wanted to, in French or Italian, all the same gibberish to me. See the thing was I knew where Father L. kept the stuff.

I was always the first alter boy to arrive. Mom wanted me to get there early, so I'd be the one to light the candles. So I'd be the one to ring the bells at that magical moment. So I be the one issuing in the transformation, the invisible weirdness of God, and she, sitting in the front row, dead center, with her white bouffant halo of hair, could have a major part in the mystery. I was her little helper of Christ. Her connection to the revolving spheres. Her little priest-in-the-making. Priest boy with a dirty collar. And high-top Converses. Black and white, though.

The fathers lived their solitary lives in a modern rectory right beside the church. It was connected by a walkway that led into the mass preparation room, really a kitchen with closets. In the closets were the altar boys' garbs: black robes on hangers and a cloud of the white ballooning outer garment. We called them para-t-shirts, all a size way too big. In that room there was a sink, cupboards, a refrigerator, a wall pegged and hung like pool cues with candle lighter/snuffers, and a bathroom with stainless steel fixtures.

One of the first duties, after suiting up, was to fill the wine and water holders. Two ceramic mugs that are taken from the back of the church, down the main aisle, up to the altar, it's . . . communion time, when the sunlight is streaming in through the stained glass as glorious and radiant as movie projector light, the chimes *jingjingjingling*, the mixed water and wine are united into hemoglobin of the Lord. Yeah. And, amen.

There were two bottles. One of white grape juice. One of the dark stuff. To me it looked like blood already. I filled the wine mug up twice as much as Father L. wanted. It was 7:15 in the morning, still night outside. In the hall that led to the entrance of the church, I drank half of it.

It was rank. It made me burp. It made a pool of spit in my mouth. I ran back into the bathroom to see my nose swell up and turn red. It didn't. But I had the cheeks of a girl. A pretty girl. A cherub in disguise.

I don't remember serving that mass, not really. I almost fell asleep, but Henry, my partner, my assistant altar boy, kicked me in the leg so

I hit the chimes on cue. What I do remember is staring at the wood carved stations of the cross on the wall and thinking that each one of those Jesuses has a different face. Each of the Jesuses' wood slit eyes were looking right at me. He—they didn't seemed pissed. He was aware. He was aware that I wanted his blood. He was telling me this was a good thing. He was looking at me, occasionally blinking a woodcut eyelid. Click. Click.

The cross wasn't so heavy to carry. The people's faces in the crowd were not so intimidating. How the ring on Father L.'s finger glistened in the stained glass light. How his nose shone like a clown's. How Sister Marie hair struggled to get out of her habit in wild locks of auburn. How Sister Marie wasn't a mom, how she never would be one. How Sister Marie sitting devoutly in the first row, opposite side of the church as my mom, Sister Marie who was underneath her white gown something like a real woman. I guess?

I found my religion in that first morning sip of wine. All I needed, logically, was followers.

~

Mass usually went like this. We walked out among the masses, the congregation. I carried the crucifix on its long wooden stick. I held Christ on his cross for a captive audience. I had power and I liked it. I was the priest's best man. People aligned themselves in pews. All kinds of people, mostly older people, dressed finely. There were women waiting to take a bite out of His body, to taste a sip of His blood. There were young women. Waiting and ready for us, Jesus' middlemen. First, they had to get through us.

Waiting to be taken to a higher level is what we all want. It's what the faceless congregation wanted. Weird, how I knew them, by face, after mass, but when they were in there, just a crowd. Rocking back and forth. Solemn even when they were singing. One day I could take them there, to wherever they wanted to go, I just knew it. It's what every parable of the Bible said when I read them. Assigned reading. So short the stories. But lessons so long.

One day I would have followers of my own religion maybe. One day I would grow into that Nordic portrait of Christ my mother had hanging in her house, her bedroom, her bathroom, her garage. If I could ever grow a beard and moustache. One day I would be a holy Bjorn Borg.

After mass, after we cleaned up, put back the containers of holiness, extinguished the candles, and with our own static halos of fuzz head we got from quickly pulling off our vestments, we'd talk in the empty church. We the altar boys. We'd talk about this: altering girls in all kinds of different ways.

See, there is this idea about Catholic girls. That they are all vixens beneath their patterned, checkered skirts. That they paint their toenails red and even dark brown, their little perfect toesies hidden in the ugliness of saddle shoes. That beneath their white blouses, their still growing boobs ached to burst from their tight starter bras. That within their braided strands of blond or black (or both) hair were thoughts. Dark thoughts. Gothic thoughts. That they were the brides-in-waiting of Christ, just like the nuns. Vestal virgins in a time when only religion, their religion, was holding them back.

Wasn't true at all. They were just normal kids, like everyone else. Really, they were just like us boys. Well, except for Marybeth. She fit the bill. She was different. She had one very favorable quality. Um, well, she liked me.

Marybeth didn't look like a Catholic girl at all. I don't mean she didn't dress the dress, she did, she wore her uniform just like all the others. Fashion was never an issue at St. Vincent's, guarded by the strict rules of school. But she'd do things like unbutton the first two buttons of her shirt when the nuns weren't around. The other teachers, the civilians as we called them, the not-nuns, wouldn't pick up on these things, so they never corrected her. But boys knew what it meant. She was open to things. She had a big heart. Like the sacred heart of Jesus, bared to all and burning with flames of love. Hey, it was on every scapular to see, His sacred heart. His guts exposed like in the invisible man model in the science room.

Marybeth had brown reddish hair, like a middle-eastern maiden. Like Veronica. She had mysterious beauty marks too. One above her lip, just like a woman was supposed to. A movie star. And she had a few on her cheeks. She had a cute round nose, she had thick red lips that she painted with cherry-scented gloss. She shaved her legs above the knee. She painted her fingernails clear.

It was a Friday afternoon in the month of March that Sister Christina marched us all into the church that was across the school's massive freshly blacktopped parking lot to attend dreaded confession. The weather had begun to be spring-like and our class, 7-1, exploded into open air. We ran in and out of the yellow lines of parking places. We grabbed at blossoms budding from tips of trees. Sister C. didn't mind. She wasn't in it for the control. She was a nun because, we speculated, she never had a man and she wanted children and we were them. Our break into the freedom of a cool breezy day was tainted though. Our destination was the dark, gloomy church that always smelled like horrible incense. We were to make our confessions in a new style. Confession day. The way to do it was something our elders were calling "face to face".

No more portable johns of the confessional booth. Smelling of varnish, dark with screens, scented with naughty secrets. A trend had happened in the Church. Rolling with the changes. We, as novice sinners, were to face the priest, one on one.

Forgive me Father for I have lied to you?

Adolescent boys and girls, oozing with the juices of adulthood, temptation, speaking directly to the priest, the resident godhead. They told us to tell him the truth.

The truth?

Right!

Anything but the gospel truth. What we did was, well, lower the ante of our sins. If I had ripped off a Playboy from my brother's apartment, I'd convert it to "I have stolen a magazine". If me and a bunch of friends beat the living crap out of Jimmy the Geek or if we had thrown a soccer ball at the head of Darrell—the partially in some slight way retarded guy—many many times, although with a low rate of target connection, ball to head, then I'd say "I have hurt my fellow man." That one sounded good. It was fun to say. If we had sneaked over the Debbie M.'s on some boring Saturday afternoon to basically come on to her until she let us (we're talking three guys) fondle her breasts, then, as if that weren't enough, in a sexual energy feeding frenzy, we'd rummage through her underwear drawer because that's just something boys do. Boys are gonna do what boys do.

Forgive me Father for I have been naughty. Almost.

As it turns out, Marybeth began to check me out, to get interested. Words were passed, notes were circulated, we began to hang out together during recess. Yeah, the guys called me "faggot" for not wanting to play Kill the man with the Ball. I began to notice what she had beyond those buttons. Little round flesh nubs that had been previously concealed by her loose-fitting white overshirt. We boys began to figure out what these uniforms were for. She began leaving her top two buttons unbuttoned. All the time, even during class. Mr. Franklin didn't seem to mind. She wore what couldn't have been trainer's bra. It was blue! It had a little pink bow in the middle. It was fascinating, like a new kind of puzzle.

As most girls her age do, she worked as a babysitter. She got the job of watching the Yeaglin's kid, Timmy, a one year-old. No big problem for her, and they were pretty cool people: rich, big house, he was a doctor, she was a counselor or something. They went out a lot. They lived four blocks away from Marybeth in a nice neighborhood. It had some stupid name like Nestlingwoods.

It was Saturday night, end of March, 1980 when she invited me over. The kid was fast asleep. The house smelled like warm milk. We watched tv together. We played records on their stereo. We took our shoes off. We cuddled. We kissed. We kissed French. Her tongue was disgusting: bumpy, cool, wet of course but even kind of slimy. I cut my tongue on her braces. It hurt.

We learned how to kiss each other, another. We felt where we weren't supposed to feel. It was weird. She grabbed it, through my pants. She rubbed. She rubbed hard. I had to stop her. She was going to rub the skin right off it! I did the same for her but there kind of wasn't anything there, except for warm. Really warm. Hot warm.

Like an explosion, a super novae, I was off of her when we heard the door's lock click from upstairs. *They were home early.*

Something must have gone wrong. We both screamed!!! Adreneline rush of gulit.

All I remember is the smell of her lip gloss in my nostrils, two very surprised looking individuals of the parent type as I sprinted from the louvered window laundry closet, tripped up the red carpeted stairs, and let the door bonk open, my identity I hoped read blur.

Just like a boy. A boy with balls who didn't know what to do with them.

That was pretty much the end of the story. We felt too weird about getting caught. We felt like sinners. She ended up getting the better of me. Freshman year of high school I benched on the varsity soccer team. I got a varsity letter for it, so I bought a jacket. One cool night at a football game I let her wear it, her heart pounding under my proudly displayed "R" that my mom sewed on. . . I never got it back. Never did find out the secrets about her I wanted. What a naked body meant. What she really smelled like.

On Sunday morning, I would have to do the eight o'clock mass. But back to the escape, that night of epiphany. After the big ditch that separated Tanglewood from Northmoor, then from my neighborhood, that scurrilous Saturday evening, I beelined for the rooted out oak stump.

In it we kept a fifth of whatever we could swipe from somebody's Dad's liquor cabinet. Overlooking the banks of the neighborhood creek, a place we called Frankenstein's grave because the concrete substructure all broken up now looked like a crypt or a bunch of fallen tombstones, I drank for the first time alone. I drank not in church.

I drank looking at trees and a thin rivulet of floating water and listening to raccoons rustling in the undergrowth and I thought: well this must be it. This was what it all was about and would always be. The world was nothing except what I made it out to be. I would float through life with bells ringing in the back of my head. I would transform drink into my own blood. My life was a church of dreams. I drank myself to sleep. Woke up whenever way too late at night, ran home, snuck into bed.

At mass in the morning, at least I wasn't tempted to hit the wine on Sunday. My head throbbed. I felt sick, but it was a sick that couldn't be cured by anyone but myself. Henry tried to get me to have a few sips. It smelled rank.

"C'mon," he said, "before Father's done shaving."

In the bathroom down the carpeted hall we could hear the faucet on and a vague smell of cheap aftershave. My little hangover that wasn't painful, I could still kind of think, so I declined. He called me a pussy and downed a quarter of the bottle while I went out, in full regalia and Converse hightops to light the candles. When I came back, Henry burped loud. The congregation probably didn't hear because of the piped in organ music & electronic bells ringing in the tower.

Father L. came out of the bathroom, dressed, nodded to us.

"It's time, my little saints."

We nodded. Coogan took the water and wine. Father L. handed me the crucifix. I led the procession to the altar.

With the glistening body of Christ, crucified, over my head, my pounding head, and what I knew to be the world around me waiting for my one genuflection, my mom staring at me with one eye cocked open, and in moments, moments left up to me that would start the ball of worship rolling, I walked confident positive for the first time ever, I too would never ever ever die.

ME AND HER AND MY MACHINE

Blinking red eye. The blinking red eye. How he dreaded it. Like in that crazy Poe story. The one about this man and he's, well, living with this other guy, and, now, how does it go? And so anyway he gets real pissed off at this guy 'cause this guy has this eyeball that's milky white gross and so this other guy, like, slices him up, and well, you get it. Quite logical if you think about it. For a while.

But what can you do to a machine? A machine with a blinking red eye. A fucking twenty buck heaping crap of technology you bought from a derelict at a pawner's who had missing bottom teeth and cologne that smelled like sweat. A little black box of a machine that's got something on you—that knows a little bit about your eventual future, knows who you hang with. A machine that has some vital information someone else has entrusted to it, and not you. An answering machine that never not once answers to you.

I hate these things and so do you. Everyone does. They're the price we pay for living in modern times. We need so bad to catch all possible information, invitations to parties, possible job leads, romantic intrigues of friends and co-workers. Any bit of information that tells us something about us or who we want to be. Any possible reflection of ourselves. Narcissus with technologies. Narcissus in a Hall of Mirrors.

You sit there like an idiot, alone in a room, after three hours of trying how to figure out how to record a message, and when you finally do, then you dread the deed. It's like cuddling in public. There are better times and places. One on one. Your worst date—you and yourself. Duration: sixty seconds.

What makes it so bad is that you're on the spot with yourself. You fuck up—you stutter, you mispronounce—and you have to do it all over again. Like being your own blind date on a mutually bad night.

You and you in secret conversation. Overheard only by yourselves.

Who doesn't despise their own voice played back on tape? All day long, you walk around the halls at work, sifting some Sinatra tune from your gut through your teeth into the air. Thinking the ladies are melting in their seats, you trill those vocal chords at others assured that the organ music emitted from your pipes is wholly an original, mellifluous song. (Note: you have practiced how to say mellifluous).

You yourself a Benedict Arnold of spontaneity who rehearses what amounts to be almost prescribed messages to friends and beloveds in what you have cleverly learned to be named dulcet tones, describing your exact state of mind and mental/spiritual bearing (that have oftentimes been cut of by a rude beeping), but regardless of all this, you never think that of the betrayal done to all your grandiose croonings by the rare instrument of your throat until that very moment that all of life stops, as you press the playback button and sit silently, open-mouthed in denial hear the seal in heat croup.

You hate the way you sound. If only you recorded yourself having sex! And maybe even watched it in slo-mo.

Then there's the rhetorical problem. The message. What should it say, exactly. Should there be funky music in the background, the James Bond theme, or classical, the sound of a busy city and people mumbling "peas and carrots, carrots and peas?" No one knows. But everyone thinks about it. More than once.

Should it just be you—your voice—the humm of electricity—a confession presided over by the priest of reality? How does it go?

beep

"Hello, this is Pete's machine answering because Pete isn't here ..."

beep

Why the hello?

"Hi, this is (#). Please leave a message."

A robot with an electronic soul. Too informal. Too—*I am not a number! I'm a man!* And why the *please*. This type of message solicits a lot of messages from wrong number callers anyway. Never worth the listening. People are so sure they're calling who they want to call. They choke up in disbelief that they've screwed up. How could the telephone lie? How could they misdial? Technology can always be trusted. Technology never means to let us down.

So there's no way to actually go about it. Strange the wrong messages left on a machine. These are great to listen to, probably because the people are prepared and it's their choice if they leave a message or not. Those who need to reveal something about their personality. A dollop of them. A pause you'd never want to interrupt. A catch in the throat that signals vulnerability.

beep

"Misses Jackson, you left your wallet in the pocket of your dry cleaning. We put it in a bag under the counter so you can come in and pick it up. It looks like a wallet, but we didn't open it, so we're not so sure what in it. It is here though, so you an pick it up whenever. Your pocketbook that is."

You got to believe it.

The reason why I'm even going into all of this is because I do not know what to do. The tv's playing, birds are chirping outside even though it night, I'm messed up and the phone is in my hand. My brain is dancing to that dialtone tune, that little tornado warning that the line makes after the dialtone has hung up on you.

"*eeeeeeeeeeeeeeeeeeeeeeeeeeeeeeeeeeeeeeee*"

It began when she left this message I recorded onto a microcassette recorder. I listen to it periodically. I have a lot of these tapes. They keep me busy. Anyway, hers kinda goes like:

beep

"*mmmmmm-ello,*(tune humming in background) thought you'd be (deeply seductive intake of breath) . . . *home. But you're not and that's* (pouty baby voice) *oh so too too bad.*"

After I heard this I fumbled through the receipts that I keep and invariably lose when it comes to checkbook balancing time. I ripped through my wallet to find that piece of napkin or tear of post-it-note that I wrote her number on. God is willing and I find it. I called her back. I get her machine.

Her voice is as sultry on her message as it is on my machine. She sounds good recorded. How can this be so?

It beeps.

I hang up.

I'm not one for phone tag.

I call back immediately. Busy. Her machine is thinking to itself.

I wait five minutes. Ring.

beep

"Hey, what's going on? Got your message. Now it's your turn to call. Thought maybe we could hook up, hang out, have ourselves a time. Call me back."

Yeah, I practiced it a few times in my head before I said it. So it would come out nice and smooth. So it would leave little waves of reverberation that would cause her fingers to move and her throat to tremble and the creases underneath her breasts to sweat as she phones me back. Ready. Willing. Eager.

It doesn't happen for days.

When I do finally get her message, it goes something like this. And, oh, I didn't re-record this one.

"Hey, what's up? Didn't get your message until too late to get back with you. If you want to go out, or something, I'm going to be at the Massachusetts' happy hour on Friday. With some friends. Be there. We'll talk for real."

The Massachusetts is this kind of preppy bar downtown where people go to be seen. Drinks there are real expensive. The women there are mostly beautiful. Sometimes they smoke cigars. The guys there are all assholes. Sometimes they smoke cigars, too. The other thing that freaks me out is it's name. I don't know why it's called the Massachusetts even though I should.

This is a day later. I call her in the afternoon. I leave her this one:

"O.k., hi and everything. That bar thing sounds all right if I can get away at that time. Hope your friends are as pretty as you. See you then."

Guess what? I never went.

It just wasn't my kind of place. I mean, you got to feel right about where you are for things to happen, if you know what I mean. I don't even know what that place's jukebox has on it—probably Bananarama and select soul tunes thrown in for flavor. I don't even know if it has a jukebox. What's a guy to do?

A couple of days later I call her back. I get the machine. I freeze up. I get paranoid. I start thinking she has caller ID and is avoiding me. But I think, hey, she gave me her number. She wrote it down on a something or other. Does it get more official than that? Wasn't a drunken ink bleeding scrawl on some cheap dive's sorry ass excuse of a napkin the classic intro? Or maybe I'm dreaming this. Maybe she wrote it down on a bus ticket. A matchbook, a movie stub, an invitation to a party she never went to.

Maybe she was being polite. Democratic and all. Maybe she collects phone messages. Oh what I wouldn't do for her machine's secret code. So in the privacy of my own mental womb, I could dial her up, plug in that number, and surf through her other messages.

beep

"Yes, hullo, this is Dale the plumber. Can you call me back so I know when's the best time I can drop by to check out your pipes? Thank ya."

beep

"Hi honey, this is Mom. Was returning your call of, oh let's see, Thursday evening. Hope everything's all right. Love you."

beep

"Hey baby, it's Charles. Last night was out of sight. Did I leave my belt there? Call me."

beep

" Girl this is Rosalee. Did that guy ever get back to you? How was he? He isn't gay. I mean, he seemed so nice and all. You never know. Calling to let you know that if you aren't interested in him, I might be. Talk to me."

Nah, it couldn't be like that. She doesn't seem like that kind. I mean, she wears braids. She uses clear nail polish. Am I getting my signals crossed, or what?

I dial her up again. I know she must know that it is me calling and hanging up but I'm hoping that her machine doesn't record me hanging up (it's not like I'm breathing hard) and I do, can time my click with quartz-like precision.

beep

"Me again. Hoping you know me now by voice. We got to get together soon. You must be busy working, or I hope nothing's come up. Give me a call. I should be around most of today and tomorrow. Number is 321-8868. Bye."

Couldn't be more straightforward than that. What I will do is wait. I won't hang out. I'll stay home. She'll call. We'll go out. I'll see where she's coming from. We'll go out for a bite. We'll get a drink. She will see that I'm more than a nasally voice badly taped. She'll hear that my voice is song. She'll get addicted to that tune. We will get it on. When other men call her number in the future, they'll get me on the message machine.

beep

"Hi, we're out right now. We'll get back to you. Message us."

But it never happens this way, does it? Never except in lame movies.

She calls me back. She gets my message. This is how it happens.

beep

"Hey, it's me. So what is your problem? Are you afraid of me? Of yourself? You need to lighten up. I'm real busy that's all. I work my ass off. I'm trying to make my job a better one, or quit. I don't know what I'm doing. I take whatever as it comes. I hate schedules. I can't organize anything, least of all my life. I'm sorry we can't hook up. But you need to hang loose. Not be so anal. Here's something for you. To think about. *BRRAAPPPPPPP.* Click."

I was astounded. I couldn't believe it. She ripped one. One the phone. She farted on my machine! I have it taped! I play it back to my friends! It's great! God, does she have guts! She does have guts. And I've heard them!

The funny thing is is that I'm the one who's too embarrassed to call her back. Usually, people are together for years before they can share such moments. I know married couples who can't even after years. And she rips one on my phone. What the hell does it mean?

I call her back. I get her machine. I don't have to fart. I have ten seconds. I don't know what to say. I am disgusted. I am enthralled. There's no time to think.

beep

"What is up with that? More subtle ways to make a point. You did, didn't you. Listen, I'll call you back. Or I'll pick you up after work. Call me, tell me the address. Friday night. We'll do happy hour. Bye."

After hanging up, I wondered what phone sex with her might be like.

Days go by. I do nothing. I check my messages endlessly. Always some idiot calling to sell me something like life insurance, magazines, crap no one ever buys on the phone, more credit cards. I'm too afraid to call her. Ball's in her court. Or the balls.

I watch a lot of t.v. I begin drinking by myself while watching a lot of tv. I listen to music. I drink. If I had any drugs, I'd do them. I begin cooking for myself. I invent sandwiches. Bologna and fried onions with Dijon mustard. A fried ham/hamburger and bacon bits steak platter. I eat these things. I wait by the phone.

RRRRRRRRIIIINNNNGG. She calls. It must be her. It's Sunday night. I put my hand on the receiver. My machine picks up before I have the will to. It's her. There's something wrong. She's not saying anything. She's crying. She's trying to cry. She's trying to say something.

I hear heavy breathing. I hear what sounds like pain. I hear seriousness made into sound. She's struggling. She's fighting to hold something off. She's breathing, breathing harder. I recognize her breath. It's getting more difficult. She's saying something like *"ooooooooooooooooo"*. She screams as the phone cuts off, hangs up.

I'm sweaty.

I go get the bottle.

I drink.

I don't know what else to do.

I stare at the t.v. screen. There are people talking. Whatever they have to say is pointless.

A woman has phoned me.

A woman has phoned me and a woman has orgasmed on my answering machine.

And if I had picked it up?

I drink.

I drink some more.

The rationality alcohol brings makes me wonder. I'm putting two and two together. Did she have someone with her? Would she do that to me? Why would she do that to me? I don't even hardly know her. What does she want with me? Could it have been me? What should I do.

I wait five minutes. I hold the phone in my hand. I don't want her calling back. I don't want her smoking a cigarette on my machine. My machine is my machine. We share secrets. My machine knows everything about me. Now my machine knows her. She does not know me. I do not know her. But she knows something I don't.

She knows my machine.

TRANSFORMED, THE OFFICE NARCISSUS

It was the day he no longer recognized his foot that, really, everything changed. And foot, not feet, because the other one was the same as usual. Long toes, a half-moon hung in the big nail, a pinkie toe curled as a quietly sleeping fetus, nearly as long as its cousin finger, eek!

That foot, the right one, was fine. Same bald man's head heel, too.

But the other one, the left one, was somehow different. Was it from a mis-step in a tidal pool the day he thought he might have clipped an urchin? Or was it the day she got him so mad that he kicked the wall? Twice. Or was it a genetic snafu made apparent only by time's slow fuse, not noticed until now?

Who's to know these things. How was it, um, different? Well, the imprint it made on wooden floors after a shower was more—pointed. The hair on its smooth lady-like skin carapace began reddening. The toenails altogether stopped growing. A definitely higher ankle, a more profound arch. The weirdest thing was, after a long day contained in the prison of sock, it even kinda smelled different. Like it wasn't, well, *his* foot.

~

Eight thirty-seven a.m. Generic coffee a-brewing. At the office the workers began piddling in. There were three women who were definite "definites". That's to say, they are in my book, definite definites, and only in mine. I have no idea what the other teachers think for they are, number one, professionals, and two, professors, and thus their minds must remain closed-book mysteries. Everyone knows they really don't have personalities. And that is why they are teachers. They know nothing.

From time to time, perhaps in the lunchroom or in the elevator, even in the echo chamber that is the stairwell, one of them might mention a student by name. Just the name, the moniker. Never even a hint of a glance, nor a gesture, that might reveal a subtext of a reference or a splinter of meaning, and if they do reveal something it is for those who have already figured them out. Or a human, soul-inspired line might be offered to a fellow teacher or student of a youngish nature who is/are however non-ironically also, of an extremely beautiful nature, and well, all in all, in nothing ever really said.

Back to the matter at hand. There are three very definite definites.

Some simple questions are just that. Take for instance how some people stay extremely fit. They eat a lot of fish. Perhaps mainly of sushi-based diet. Or, say, fish cooked in the oven, or salmon smoked, the occasional oyster, mussel, abalone, and as much raw shrimp as possible. To make the mind sharp or to keep the fat off the important places. The places others need to grab and hold on to. But forgive me. I'm doing what I am paid to do. I am endlessly digressing.

~

Having a different foot is not a crisis in itself. At least not publicly. Shoes conceal many things. Including hygiene. What one considers sexy and how they take care if its leads to this thing we call appeal. Maybe it's in the fact of knowing a part of you, of your anatomy, is all of a sudden one day, changed. Revelations the shower brings. But how to appeal a change?

Everything changes. Food begins to be a particularly picky affair. No longer can your mouth sink into a perfectly grilled T-bone, rainbow red in the middle, in a pool of its own sanguine juices, on an extra large plate heaped with the cuttings of grilled vegetables. Not when you are trying to, like the Japanese, stay extremely fit.

Nothing tastes the same. Not even the basics. The cool, sweet draw of a glass of creamy vitamin D milk. Not even the crisp retort of a baguette bitten into fresh from a bakery. Not even the elixir of a glass of artesian tap water. Not when your foot has changed into that of another's.

What else does one need than definite definites? Of course it sounds bad. Most propositions do at first. But taken into context, it begins to make sense. Sense in the way one absolutely has to look at life. Life and its options. And the options on the options.

Sheree is just that type of person. You know, the type that dresses, or shall we be frank and say overdresses, as the classy kind of woman she reveres and not so secretly wants to be. Right down, or up to the hippest Italian made frames and lenses, the most stylish little ensembles she can pick up at the outlet (nobody knows), and the latest of the latest shoes that grace her manicured feet like perfectly fitting leather rickshaws. At least some people's parts never change.

Sheree the spite of the photocopier where she always is, cheerfully. Perusing through a book, mentioning the weather, not saying much to anyone although greeting and chatting with an equal degree of sincerity and kindness. She wears lip gloss, her hair up or down, both as devastatingly seductive as she herself knew it to be, and a perfume that will only allow itself to be described as honeysuckle in the rain.

~

There aren't enough windows in any building anytime a looking-out-of-the-window-feeling comes. No groovy tree-shaded grove with an Akita tied to one of its trunks. A bus *psssshhhhhtttiinnnnggg* by and dropping off four black ladies wearing similar hats on a day that just about everybody's car is broken down, probably a dead battery, and a long a long crack in the window, a fifty-pound sack of birdseed in the trunk. Windows to the outside which clouds form in for moments in time asking for someone, anyone to think of them and their shapes as giant, cottony ducks.

How come nobody wonders if ghosts get hungry.

~

Reenita was the sun rising anywhere but the tropics, unless from under needles of palm trees. She was nothing that words can in anyway describe so why not then try? It's like this—cat or mouse—we're either after fur or bait. She was a teacher of the Romantics, the Victorians, the Elizabethans, literary anyones who were literally anyones. She was a Queen of lineage purely intellectual, a pure-blooded Yale-ian, Oxfordian, Sorbonnianne and this is how she carried herself wearing the requisite facial expression.

This is what Reenita expects: be nice to her or leave the room. Hold open the door if she is leaving or entering. Offer to make her a cup of coffee or tea. Instruct her patiently and clearly, and lovingly, on how to send a fax. Do not attempt to get to know her deep enough that you'll be able to guess one of her favorite wines. Do not attempt to learn what she, herself, living human flesh and blood, really thinks of Shelley's tear-stained letter or why she wears like clockwork sheer panty hose with the line down the back.

~

Camera pans in from the Superstition Mountains of all places Arizona, fast time, over the yellow blooming bushy heads of a forest of palos verdes, like a cruise missile mis-fired. Towards a city, first a white-line on the horizon, then some rooftop, then the micro-chipped, electronic card design of a planned suburb to crash and crash just over spouts of water shot into the air by a group of mating whales into the Pacific Ocean. Smart bomb camera tv out. A flicker. Then, blackness.

Finally one day a decision will have to be made. A commitment. You will have to sit down and accept the fact that the place that surrounds you is where you live and where you, geographically and mentally, are. You have willingly chosen a certain package of clichés, a locality with certain options and lack of them, a story book setting from a best-seller only you will read. A river city with a slow moving swell, big shade trees, young people bicycling by, false bistros, a walkway made for promenading that no one uses, a city in which the food's so good everybody eats out.

Or it'll be a small mountain town with great water. Ski resorts surrounding, a mix of wealthy inhabitants and not rich locals mostly deriving from Scandinavian midwestern stock, great shopping and a brick-paved outdoor mall where people get together to eat and drink and get drunk and even watch performances of themselves provided by street actors.

Or it'll be the anonymity of a gigantic city where everything is believed in, sampled, used and re-used, phone numbers written on shirtsleeves or bar tabs. One great big park where everyone brings their pet, acting as gauchos without style or pinache or a reckoning of the slave/master relationship. Who's the boss of the boss? And designer leashes hold who in check, willingly.

When the city that is just right even down to the stylized decal on police cars, the mortgage cleansed, and the white fence boldly painted blue or magenta, the indoor/outdoor lighting and flower beds complimentarized, you disappear. Once and forever.

~

Well, luckily, she would never leave the opportunity to view the renewing, slowly changing "We". She indeed would never see my, and I beg your pardon, lint free innie gradually extend to a little fleshy tower of babel extended. When hair begins to grow on your body, thicker, more wirey and in places and in patterns never before experienced by the angles of your particularly under-regarded but never steady best pal of a skeleton. Sometimes one says things that are not meant to be meant.

~

Today, nothing much different. I feel, maybe, it's the teeth. Maybe my teeth are changing. A tighter bite. More yellowed, probably from smoking after lunch break, which I apparently do not do. Not until tomorrow's craving. A wider expanse of arse, but firmer. A smaller stomach that has the taste for vegetable dishes and exotic cheeses. One of the lungs is still the same. Thicker nipples. Unrecognizable forearms and hands that dry easier with one of them sporting two rings that have nothing to do with marriage. The same throat and voice but the tongue seems stuck always with the bad aftertaste of chicken gizzards or cheap white wine. It is changing over. My eyes, well I've never been able to recognize them anyway so who's to say? Hair, face, lips, earlobes, chin– all are broadening. The mind. One always changes her mind.

I, you see by now, am the third office woman. Definitely.

I still go on having the most impossible and not very seemly love affairs.
—Van Gogh

HOW HIGH THE MOON

The dingy white carpeting is stained in what seems to be blood or years of tea spillage & yet she asks me to take off my shoes. She is Japanese. I should have worn better socks. She is the most beautiful woman I have ever seen. My socks are a gray that matches the carpeting.

I am a simple Midwestern boy. What I am doing in a third story walk up in the lower Haight is beyond immediate understanding. I have been lifted by a force, by aliens, by un-understanding and deposited in someone's acid 1970s hungover, post-sex dream only without the acid. And the sex.

Across the street, the Arabic shop owner will give you a free American Spirit if you ask. His store has everything. It has booze and ice cream and duct tape.

Her hair is a raven that has been lost in the wilds for 14 years. She is from a southern island of Nippon. Shikashima, near Fukuoaka, where the women are known to be fiery, stubborn, much like the mindset that gave birth to kamikaze pilots. The most skilled ones are purportedly from her part of the world.

She, as one might envision, is not rail-thin skinny. C cups. She actually has a butt. I cannot ethically tell you her name, it just wouldn't be right, but it is beautiful and it rhymes with yo-yo. Crème-colored skin, ample lips, a voice like a bird whose wings were once clipped, eyes like jewelry a shark might don, big feet for a girl, and a respectable five foot five.

My ABJ friend Ted tells me that we all go through our J-girl phase just as they all go through their blond haired blue-eyed boy phase. My eyes are green—something I can forgive him for missing. He's right. He's wrong. I can't get over her.

At this moment I am tempted to see out the AVIs on my laptop that I have recorded of her. Her speaking to friends on Skype. Her friends who summed me up as if I were a cut of beef, appraising my looks, my facial features, my build, my height. I must admit something: I like being a piece of meat.

You get to that point of life in which you realize that it is all just a large bad oil painting you are sitting for, one day to remain unsold at a staving artists' fair at a local Ramada Inn and there is nothing more to do than try to look pretty and try to enjoy the swaths of brushstrokes. My eyebrows are pointy like Jack Nicholson's.

And broad brushstrokes at that. The carpeting that was once white and now some insidious shade of not exactly white nor gray is so saturated in mistakes that it looks like a monochrome Twister mat. I was beside myself when she asked me to remove my shoes because they are not clean.

Soon we will be twisting ourselves in lustful origami is the only thought that comes to my mind. And somehow I will be able to perform in some quasi-Asiatic way that conforms to her idea of romance that will calm her cat-like eyes. Ah, the simple priorities of men.

Not a drinker of beer other than Kirin or Sapporo, I have nevertheless convinced her that 2 bottles of Pinot Grigio will quell her desire for a flavored saki-type buzz. Like a fly trapped in a windowless room she does like to buzz unless it is in the confines of non-public places. I notice that all the paper shades are drawn.

Yet, this is better than where I ended up last week. When a marriage ends, and divorce rears its Hydra head, and the woman you dedicated your life to for 23 years walks out, with the dog, let me tell you, Donne's compass is fucking broken. The story I will never write is the one in which I am in a house under the BART tracks in Cherryland with what turned out to be a gorgeous tweaker. I do not know how exactly. I met this radiant blonde with big puppy dog eyes on the sidewalk patio of the Bistro. She had bags and bags of groceries with her. I offered her a ride home, eyes glued resolutely to her cleavage. Oh how when boobs are taken away, the drive to replace them is purely genetic and infantile.

It was only until we got into the rational light of the IHOP (nothing else was open at 1:30 a.m.) that I could tell that there was something twittery about her. Her eyes, of course. Sunken and unreal. Blank. Desperate and lizard-like, just like my libido.

She wasn't crazy just sad. And the meth hadn't evaporated her body yet. Tan, she was. With soapy skin.

But back to scene I, act 2. The Filmore Street apartment was nothing more than an attempt at white paint painted over dirt and a few plants, a plank at the entrance of her room to forestall the advances of a mouse, nothing on the walls but wall, shoes aligned in the hallway. My new shot in the dark with eastern sun rising was quite the opposite. No drugs ever. Thirty-sixish. Marijuana confused and frightened her.

The refrigerator was stocked with inscrutable Asian products the kind we Westerners would have absolutely no idea what to do with. I swear I saw a value-pak of nato. Just the thought of opening that for breakfast with a raging hangover brings up the smile of bile.

Her room—like someone planning to go on a long trip. Total random attempt at organization, of course the sleeping mat on the floor, boxes of perfume and lotions, jewelry on small tables amassed like pirate's booty. The overall sense of always being in a rush. Some travel books indicating destinations desired. Everything in flux and at the same time so static.

Sweet or some would say semi-pretty view out the window behind the cheap Venetian blinds backed by paper shades that could never be pulled up for fear that some pervert might be watching her from other apartments, from the street fifty feet below, waiting for the exact pose that could give them gratification or a murderous inclination. Voyeuristic spasms. A painting covered of the north slope of Twin Peaks, torn cotton blouses of fog spinning from its spinach-covered teeth.

I simply should have known. I simply should have known it would come to this. Dates in which I buy her flowers, show her the best eateries such as the Italian place in Potrero from which the fabled city lights twinkle in the immediate distance. Where she ordered a Riesling and then complained about its sweetness not knowing it tasted that way because she paired it with a salty shrimp risotto. I could only look out the window through the letters painted backwards on the glass in brown and wonder why my dream life, why my personal Woody Allen movie was going so very off script.

Television image in my mind: Godzilla rising from the sea. Screaming that Godzilla-y scream. Puppet gestures. The Tokyo of my emotions in flames.

Somebody orders something in Italian. A woman in a trench coat appears in the door. Glorious distractions.

I take her home after the ambiguous dinner. After flavored saké, peach it might have been, that she had procured especially for me/ us, she takes me into her lair and I notice the tour guide books of the desert U.S.A. & the Southwest stacked in a corner. Her hair is not hair that I have ever known, like a horse's mane sort of, like a synthetic fabric, like the bristles, long of course, shoulder length, of a shaving brush, yes softer, ut in a way, similar. Her skin to me is Mediterranean, her nails are perfect slices of petrified almonds, and she has no smell not even where she should and when she should and we are somehow together, quickly, entwined. Shangri-la on Filmore at two a.m.

Until she tries to touch me with intention.

A fish stroking its gills against your belly. A small jolt of electrical current while unplugging the hairdryer. A fake punch in which you can feel some anger. She did not now how to touch another because no one had ever touched her in a way that she could learn from. Like a stripper going in for a bulge tug, this is how her hand was: greedy. Sharp. Pointed. Aggressive. Needy.

It was desperation and not lust. It was premeditated and not improvised. It was somehow the opposite of what desire should feel like.

Beyond anything I could have ever believed in my life, I did something wholly not in my character. I refused to have sex with a beautiful other.

Monogamy is a bitch. Since I had been with only one woman for 20 years of my sexual life, using a condom became a conundrum. Hadn't even used one in high school due to a Catholic school upbringing and the lust for stupid danger. My walk of shame was that little prance into the bathroom. The ripping open of the package with my teeth. The assault of the disgusting chemical smell and taste of industrial strength lube. To put one's tool into a sausage casing. It just wasn't going to happen. Instant hard off.

The bathroom with its one damp washcloth next to the sink. What did it mean. The window open, exposing an inner part of the building, with vents and pipes. Looking down, people's dropped toothbrushes.

Not even the vision of her ample breasts could stir the beast within once the sacrament of the condom donning had occurred. When I attempted to mount her on my lap, grow grow the rushes grow, it just couldn't happen. Downpours of guilt. I am cheating on a woman who left me. I'm that dumbly loyal.

She wondered what was wrong. She internalized the situation to be of her own undoing, thus, resorted to insult. Really, no other had had a problem in this arena with her. She told me I wasn't a real man.

So I did something people resolutely tell me was a bad thing but to this day I have no regrets.

I had to. She forced the card. An ace in the hole. I left the room, lights miming supernovae behind the paper enshrouded window, and I broke out my laptop.

As I am a man, I had my own porn downloaded from tapes I made of myself and my true love. Quicktime movies of me carnally satisfying my beloved. And there were sound effects. It wasn't me making most of the noise.

I forced her to listen. But note this: only listen, not watch.

I pressed the sideways play triangle.

Lights, camera, action.

Sound.

She was mortified. Her eyes widened. She stood up straight. She walked out of the room. She picked up my bag and escorted me to the door.

Mission accomplished.

On the long drive home, she called me. The phone chimed mid-way through my exodus on the Bay Bridge, the moon full and low slung, waxing through a subtle gauze of brume.

She said these words to me "I do not now if you can see what I see. It is so beautiful. Open your eyes and look at the sky."

She had opened her shade. The moon was ours, a parting gift of sorts.

The city looked like a backdrop from some cornstalk theater production of a film noir and shook in my rearview mirror. A cardboard cutout illuminated with dime store Christmas lights with its boxes all aligned towards the highpoint of one single needle. It oozed blackness. It was painted the color of lonely.

And that's when I realized it. Something I had always known.

I wanted to fuck the city. Not her.

The city with its impossible to count and remember hills, its labyrinths of possibility & excellent little restaurants that had not yet become write ups in glossy magazines people read on airplanes, the sultry swaying of its bridges like ocean powered metronomes, its insanely beautiful people all who know the basics of at least two foreign languages, its shops full of stuff I could never in three lifetimes afford, its views that are so postcard that you have to look away for fear of becoming a person in a calendar or dollar store picture frame, its homeless people who are our wandering Sadhus no one ever solicits advice from, its Chinese markets that are souks of no personal space whatsoever, its Tenderloin that is an Abu Graib of desire, its seedy strip clubs full of klutzy, thigh-bruised girls all named Jezebel, its museums that are strip clubs of the mind with much more decadent knick knacks, its sadness vortexed in a giant swirl of want turned need that the pigeons know is good good eating.

So fuck you YoYo kindly and fuck you San Francisco.

Only because I cannot.

About the Author

Philip Kobylarz is an itinerant teacher of the language arts and writer of fiction, poetry, book reviews, and essays. He has worked as a journalist, a film critic, a veterinarian's assistant, a deliverer of furniture, and an ascetic. He currently teaches at Santa Clara University, Notre Dame de Namur, and Menlo College. His work appears in such publications as *Paris Review*, *Poetry*, *The Best American Poetry* series, *Massachusetts Review*, and *Lalitamba*. His first book, Zen-inspired poems concerning life in the south of France, is entitled *rues*. He lives ever so temporarily in the east bay of San Francisco.

www.ingramcontent.com/pod-product-compliance
Lightning Source LLC
Chambersburg PA
CBHW022006080426
42733CB00007B/498

* 9 7 8 1 4 2 1 8 8 6 9 3 0 *